Calenda

A play

Tim Firth

Samuel French — London
www.samuelfrench-london.co.uk

CALENDAR GIRLS

First presented by David Pugh Ltd at Chichester Festival Theatre, on 5th September 2008. The play transferred to the Noël Coward Theatre, London, on 4th April 2009, with the following cast of characters:

Cora	Elaine C Smith
Chris	Lynda Bellingham
Annie	Patricia Hodge
Jessie	Siân Phillips
Celia	Gaynor Faye
Ruth	Julia Hills
Marie	Brigit Forsyth
Brenda Hulse	Joan Blackham
John	Gary Lilburn
Rod	Gerard McDermott
Lady Cravenshire	Joan Blackham
Lawrence	Carl Prekopp
Elaine	Abby Francis
Liam	Carl Prekopp

Directed by Hamish McColl
Designer Robert Jones
Costume Designer Emma Williams
Lighting Designer Malcolm Rippeth
Music Steve Parry
Sound Designer John Leonard

CONTENTS

CHARACTERS

Chris, 50s
You want Chris at your party. She will talk to people she doesn't know, find things to say to fill silences and generate laughter. Part of this is because Chris is at home in crowds, holding court, being the centre of attention. Without Chris in her life, Annie would be better behaved, her life less fun. The two of them are like naughty schoolgirls. Ideal car — who cares, as long as it's a cabriolet. Ideal holiday — Algarve.

Annie, 50s
Annie will join in mischief but is at heart more conformist and less confrontational than Chris. After Chris has put a waiter's back up in the restaurant, Annie will go in and pour calm. The mischievousness Chris elicits saves Annie from being a saint. She has enough edge to be interesting, and enough salt not to be too sweet. Ideal car — who cares, as long as it's reliable. Ideal holiday — walking in English countryside.

Together these two are greater than the sum of their parts. They would be lesser humans had they not met each other. Each is spiritual mustard to the other's meat.

Cora, around 40
Cora's past is the most eclectic, her horizons broadened by having gone to college. This caused a tectonic shift with her more parochial parents. She came back to them pregnant and tail-between-legs, but Cora has too much native resilience to be downtrodden. She is the joker in the pack, but never plays the fool. Her wit is deadpan. It raises laughter in others, but rarely in herself. Her relationship with her daughter is more akin to that between Chris and Annie. Cora doesn't need to sing like a diva but must be able to sing well enough to start the show with Jerusalem and sing the snatches of other songs required. The piano keyboard can be marked up to enable her to play basic chords should she not be a player. Ideal car — who cares, as long as the sound system is loud. Ideal holiday — New York.

Jessie, late 60s/70s
Get on the right side of Jessie as a teacher and she'll be the teacher you remember for life. Get on the wrong side and you will regret every waking hour. A lover of life, Jessie doesn't bother with cosmetics — her elixir of life is bravery. Jessie goes on rollercoasters. Her husband has been with her a long time and is rarely surprised by her actions. Jessie bothers about grammar and will correct stallholders regarding their abuse of the apostrophe "s". Ideal car — strange-looking European thing which is no longer manufactured. Ideal holiday — walking in Switzerland or Angkor Wat.

Celia, age anything 35-50

The fact that Celia is in the WI is the greatest justification of its existence. A woman more at home in a department store than a church hall, she may be slightly younger than Chris or the same age, but she always feels like she's drifted in from another world. Which she has. She is particularly enamoured of Jessie, and despite the fact Jessie has very little time for most Celias of this world, there is a rebelliousness in Celia to which Jessie responds. It's what sets Celia apart from the vapid materialism of her peer group and made her defect. Ideal car — Porsche, which she has. Ideal holiday — Maldives, where she often goes.

Ruth, 40s

Ruth's journey is from the false self-confidence of the emotionally abused to the genuine self confidence of the woman happy in her own skin. Ruth is eager to please but not a rag doll, and despite being Marie's right-hand woman she is desperate to be the cartilage in the spine of the WI and keep everyone happy. She has spine herself — if she was too wet, no-one would want her around. But they do, and they feel protective of her because they sense there is something better in Ruth than her life is letting out. They are proved right. Ideal car — at the start, whatever Eddie wants; at the end, whatever she wants. Ideal holiday — at the start wherever Eddie is, at the end wherever he isn't. **The Rabbit Costume**: Ruth made this last night. It should be a cocktail of good intention and not enough time.

Marie, 50s

Marie has gradually built the current 'Marie' around herself over the years as a defence mechanism. She went to her Oz, Cheshire, and found Oz didn't want her. She came back scorched. The WI is a trophy to her, which justifies her entire existence. There is a lingering part of Marie that would love to be on that calendar. Ideal car — something German and well-valeted. Ideal holiday — a quasi-academic tour of somewhere in Persia advertised in a Sunday Supplement which she could then interminably bang on about.

John, Annie's husband, 50s

John is a human sunflower. Not a saint. Not a hero. Just the kind of man you'd want in your car when crossing America. When he dies it feels like someone somewhere turned a light off.

Rod, Chris's husband, 50s

You have to be a certain kind of guy to stick with Chris and Rod loves it. He can give back what he gets, and has a deadpan humour which has always made Chris laugh. He drinks a lot but never so much as to have a problem. He would work every hour to make his shop a success. And John was his mate, even though the relationship was originally channelled through their wives.

Lawrence, late 20s
Hesitant without being nerdy, Lawrence is a shy young man with enough wit to make a joke and enough spirit to turn up at the WI hall in the first place. When he arranges the shots he is close to female nudity but sees only the photo.

Lady Cravenshire, 60s
Lady Cravenshire really doesn't mean to be so patronizing. But the WI girls seem from another world. The world of her estate workers. **Dress:** when she makes an entrance, she must make an entrance. Largely white or cream to outplay the others, with a bigger hat than Marie. She is not a tweed-wearer. She must glide in like a galleon.

Elaine, 20s
Elaine really doesn't mean to be so patronizing. But Jessie seems from another world. The world of her gran. **Dress:** her clinical whites slice through like a knife. You feel you could cut yourself on that dress.

Liam, late 20s
Liam would like to be directing other things than photoshoots for washing powders. He's not so unprofessional as to let it show, but we can sense a slight weariness at having to deal with these women. There's a resigned patience to his actions and each smile he makes we feel is professional. For Liam, this photoshoot is a job. And not the job he wanted. **Dress:** Avoid wearing shades inside a building. If you've gone down that route, you've made the weary boy a wideboy.

Accents
The women of the real calendar in truth came from many parts of the country. Actors should resist the pressure to perform any kind of Yorkshire pyrotechnics. Nothing compromises the truth of comedy like a slavish attention to vowel-sounds and dipthongs. It will become a pebble in the shoe. If you can flatten the "a" so that giraffe no longer rhymes with scarf then that will be more than sufficient; but even that should not be championed over the intrinsic rhythm of the line. People travel. Communities are now gloriously multi-instrumental. We've had accents from Glasgow to Texas make the same part their own.

PRODUCTION NOTE

Where characters speak over the top of one another, a forward slash indicates where the overlapping speech begins.

SYNOPSIS OF SCENES

The action takes place in Knapeley village, Yorkshire, in the church hall and on top of a nearby hill (John's hill), and at the annual WI conference in London

ACT I

ACT II

Time — the present

BILLING REQUIREMENT

The following credits should appear in all programmes for the production:

Based on the Miramax motion picture by
Juliette Towhidi and Tim Firth

Such credit must be no less than 50% of the size of the credit to the Author and shall appear immediately under the Author's credit. Such credit will appear in all programmes and house boards for live stage productions of the Play. Such credit, excluding the writers' names, will also appear in all advertising in which the Author is billed (excluding the appearance of the Author's name in a critic's quote), and excluding award and congratulatory advertisements in which only the honourees are billed.

CALENDAR GIRLS was first presented by David Pugh Ltd at Chichester Festival Theatre on 5th September 2008.

CALENDAR GIRLS transferred to the Noël Coward Theatre, London on 4th April 2009.
Associate Producer: Stoneface Ltd.

AUTHOR'S NOTE

A word on nudity

As in the best traditions of vaudevillian fan dances, the art of the play's nudity lies in what is withheld. The choreography of this sequence is best described as "fabulous concealment". Should we see anything we oughtn't, the whole scene will deflate like a soufflé on which the oven door has been opened too quickly. Also beware — the music cues in the scene are vital as they maintain the build of euphoria in the room, especially over the set-up of the piano pose.

Tim Firth

REVISIONS TO THE TEXT

This edition of *Calendar Girls* has been revised by the author since its first printing in 2010. Please note that this is the definitive version which should be used in amateur performance.

MUSIC ON LOAN

Please note the music in the nude scene (the R&B version of *Jerusalem* at the end of Act I, Scene 6) is mandatory and available on loan from Samuel French Ltd. It can be downloaded from our Website (www.samuelfrench-london.co.uk) or send an A4 SAE to our librarian for a hard copy.

Other plays by Tim Firth published by
Samuel French Ltd

The End of the Food Chain
The Flint Street Nativity
A Man of Letters
Neville's Island
The Safari Party

Calendar Girls is dedicated to the real Calendar Girls,

Angela Baker, Tricia Stewart, Ros Fawcett,
Chris Clancy, Beryl Bamforth and Lynda Logan.

Also to the real John, John Baker,
the real Lawrence, Terry Logan,
and the real May Wilkinson, May Wilkinson.

ACT I

SCENE 1

The church hall, Knapeley Village, Yorkshire. Autumn

There is a piano with a stool next to it and a CD player on top of it, a coat stand with coats hung on it, shot glasses and a covered box. In it are five fir cones sitting on miniature "stools" in white "jackets" with "microphones", decorated to look like a boyband. A mirror hangs on one wall. There is a front door, a door leading to the kitchen area (off stage) and a serving hatch that open outwards from the kitchen area. There is also a megaphone, a slide projector and six chairs. A badminton court is marked out on the floor

In the black-out, a solo female voice sings "Jerusalem"

Cora (*singing*) "And did those feet in ancient time
　　　　　　　　　　Walk upon England's mountains green
　　　　　　　　　　And was the holy lamb of God
　　　　　　　　　　On England's pleasant pastures seen?"

The Lights come up to reveal a gang of women all doing the "Heaven and Earth" t'ai chi motion — following Chris, early fifties, at the front

　　　　　　　　　　"And did the countenance divine
　　　　　　　　　　Shine forth upon our clouded hills?
　　　　　　　　　　And was Jerusalem builded here
　　　　　　　　　　Among those dark satanic mills?"

Trying with varying success to copy Chris are Annie (dressed slightly more conservatively), Celia (dressed VERY expensively), Ruth (dressed VERY conservatively) and Jessie, about fifteen years older, and dressed very-nicely-thank-you for her age

　　　　　　　　　　"Bring me my bow of burning gold!
　　　　　　　　　　Bring me my arrows of desire!
　　　　　　　　　　Bring me my spear! O clouds, unfold!
　　　　　　　　　　Bring me my chariot of fire!"

> We are supposed to sing this song
> But I'm the on-ly one who is ...

Chris Cora, put a sock in it. You're ruining the atmosphere of Eastern mysticism.

Cora, an ex rock chick, sighs heavily and joins the others

(*Attempting "Eastern mysticism"*) And now-w, into t'ai chi position number one. "The Tibetan Archer". Into position number two. "The Tibetan Yak". Into position number three. "The Tibetan Yak Being Milked By The Tibetan —— "

At the attempt of this one, the girls abandon ship

Jessie			Oh for ——
Celia		(*together*)	What?
Ruth			That is NEVER t'ai chi.
Cora			"Milked"?!

Chris (*over this*) Moving into/ the ——
Annie (*louder*) Moving INTO the "Chris Reading The New Book On T'ai Chi I Bought Her." (*Doing a t'ai chi move of "throwing a book over shoulder"*) "Who needs that when I can make it all up?"
Chris I have read that book from cover to cover. On now please into the "Annie, Sharing Her Maltesers With Her Best Friend In The Cinema".

Chris mimes a rugby-style hand-off with her left hand, whilst repeatedly squirrelling mouthfuls from an imaginary pot with her right

Annie That is *such* a lie. I *always* let you have some.

The girls immediately start yakking

Jessie *Girls.*
Everyone (*ritually uttering*) Sorry, Miss Raistrick.
Jessie Into position number eight. The "Celia, Trophy Wife, Playing Golf." (*She performs a mystical mime of "drinking from a bottle"*)

Celia stops as the others follow Jessie's mime

Celia (*"you wanna fight?"*) OK. Well how about the "Jessie, Ex-Respectable Schoolteacher Outside Boots After The Wine Tasting Night"?

Jessie I told you that in strictest confidence!
Celia (*miming "hailing and falling into the street"*) "I'll get us a taxi."
Jessie *Celia.*
Ruth How about the "Cora, Single Mother, Taking A 'Breather' To Watch The Sunset"?

In instinctive union, all except Cora mime the act of "covertly smoking a cigarette"

Cora I have not had one for FOUR MONTHS.

Beat. Ruth looks around

Ruth What about me, then? Go on. Do your worst!
Chris Finally, the "Ruth — Miss Goody Two Shoes, Sucking Up To Her WI Chairman". (*Putting her hand up*) "Marie! Marie!"
Everyone (*putting their hands up, in rhythm*) "Marie! Marie!"
Ruth Oh now Chris you ALWAYS say this, and I DON'T. I REALLY — give me one example when I EVER have.

The door opens, unleashing the stern figure of Marie, an efficient, uptight early fifties

Marie Ruth, have you done the apple pies?
Ruth (*putting her hand up*) Yes, Marie. I did four.
Chris (*immediately*) Ta-daa.
Ruth No, why is that —— ?
Marie LADIES!

Decorum again

We are in NO sense ready for our harvest supper. Our guest speaker Brenda Hulse is coming up the path — (*barking instructions*) — we have no CHAIRS, Cora. No PROJECTOR, Ruth. Come ON, ladies.

Ruth moves the projector to the front of stage, facing out to the audience. The other girls take the chairs and arrange them around it

Chris, where are the flowers?
Chris Ah. Now.
Marie (*her world collapsing*) Oh Chris-s.
Chris Marie, the thing is ——
Marie You said you'd bring in leftover flowers from the shop!

Chris Yes. Well, much against the run of form, this week we actually sold some.

Marie Oh/ God —

Chris We're not in a position to turn down any sales at the moment.

Marie The thing is you *promise* these things, Chris, and you don't deliver.

Marie swoops out

Annie (*nodding to Chris*) You could put that on the side of your van. "Harper's Florists — we promise but we don't deliver."

Jessie May I just ask, is Brenda Hulse the one who gave us a talk on "the history of the tea towel"? 'Cause if so, I may have to commit hari kiri on my knitting needles.

Brenda Hulse (*off*) ... such a rush, *such* a r —— , are we in here?

Marie returns, suddenly all sweetness and light, with Brenda Hulse, a dull speaker

Marie Ladies, the slight delay was Brenda double-booked! She's hotfooted it over here from another engagement.

Brenda Hulse Yes. That's right. I was actually just down the dale at *another* Women's Institute. High Ghyll.

There's a little frisson goes round the room

Chris
Annie } (*together, sotto voce*) Boo.
Cora

Marie (*frostily*) Right, well anyway.

Brenda Hulse Amazing standard. Some of the autumn poems those ladies came up with were astonishing.

Marie As I say/ we ——

Brenda Hulse Decorated the whole hall with bulrush lanterns.

Marie (*loudly*) We did that last year. Wherever we lead, High Ghyll tends to follow.

That one killed flat. Marie turns

Ladies. For our talk this harvest we are especially privileged to welcome back Brenda, who last year gave us such a fascinating talk on the history of the tea towel.

Jessie starts to rise and get her coat

Jessie Well I'd *love* to stay, but ——

Celia and Ruth on either side of her pull her back down

Marie Brenda Hulse.

Some applause. Brenda takes the projector controls

Annie (*to Chris*) Now just shut up, OK. Whatever this is, you just shut up. I only laugh 'cause you laugh.
Chris I'm not going to laugh.
Annie No, you say that every time and then you laugh and it's ME that gets into trouble. You have to *promise* me ——
Chris (*dead serious*) I am not going to laugh.

Ruth turns off the lights

Brenda Hulse turns the projector on. A light shines from it on to the audience, as if we are sitting where the screen would be

Brenda Hulse (*attempting some theatre*) Ladies. This harvest come with me, as I invite you into the fascinating world ... of broccoli.

The light from the projector goes off and on again to indicate the picture changing

Chris instantly starts to twitch in her effort to suppress laughter

Chris (*nodding, mock "serious"*) Broccoli. Very good.
Annie (*not moving her lips*) You promisssssed ...
Brenda Hulse Broccoli has perhaps one of the most surprising lineages of any vegetable, and yet many persist in ranking it along merely with the carrot.

The light from the projector changes to orange

Or sprout.

The light changes to green

.

It is perhaps also the only vegetable rumoured to share a common ancestry with *this* man.

The light from the projector changes back to white

James Bond.

Chris controls a spasm of laughter brilliantly. Annie is shaking

(*Theatrically*) Yes, "*Cubby*" Broccoli who produced ALL the James Bond f——

The projector cuts out with a bang, making some jump. All is darkness

Marie *Oh for crying out loud — RUTH*!

Ruth leaps up and turns the lights on

Brenda, I'm SO sorry.
Brenda Hulse Has it broken?
Marie *Ruth*?
Ruth (*attending to it*) I don't know. It might be a fuse. My Eddie always says "fuse first"!
Brenda Hulse Well I can't do it without the slides.
Chris (*feigning despair*) Oh God DAMMIT.
Annie (*crying, hand over face*) Stop it-t ...
Marie Brenda, I do apologize. Perhaps instead seeing as we have you here, you wouldn't mind judging OUR harvest competition?
Brenda Hulse Of course.
Marie In which case, can you all bring your entries up?

There is an instant cross-fire of eyelines

Cora (*sotto voce*) Did you ...?

From the faces pulled, it appears no one else did

Marie This, Brenda, was a *craft* competition which I *always* used to set at my previous WI In Cheshire.

Marie looks round the group

Cora Sorry.

Annie Sorry.
Chris Sorry.
Celia Sorry.
Jessie Sorry.

Ruth, sitting, with the covered box, puts her arm up. Marie sees this disaster and battles to carry on

Marie The theme was "Most creative still life done with a fir cone on a theme of Autumn".
Ruth "Still life"? Was it?
Marie (*grittedly*) Yes.
Ruth Right. I've obviously slightly misunderstood that. I've done Westlife. (*She pulls the top off the box to reveal five large fir cones on "stools" in white "jackets" with "microphones"*)
Chris That is very good, Ruth.

One of the fir cones drops off

Is he the one who left?
Ruth Marie, I'm so sorry. It's just my Eddie's been away/ on —
Marie Brenda, I DO apologize.
Brenda Hulse Not a lot of point/ carrying on —
Marie Indeed. (*Pointedly AT the girls*) Not a lot of point.
Brenda Hulse No.
Marie Right, well the least I can offer, Brenda, is to lead you out of Knapeley by car so you don't get lost NEXT time.

Marie claps. The girls all follow. Brenda packs up. Marie turns her death-ray glare on the girls

Marie R-right, ladies. Our final agenda point is next year's calendar, which *this* year you all know is "views of local churches". Next year I thought we could go for the twelve most beautiful views —
Chris (*privately to Annie*) Of George Clooney.
Marie (*approaching the end of her tether*) — of Wharfedale Bridges, with —
Chris Eleven fully-clothed with a little "lift-the-flap" for December.

Chris capitalizes on this to Annie. Marie advances on Chris

Marie Do you have a suggestion for a calendar, Chris?

8 Calendar Girls

Chris (*quietly*) No.
Marie So "Bridges Of Wharfedale" it is then. (*Super-sweetly*) Brenda?

Marie shepherds Brenda out

There is a hangdog pause

Cora (*singing*) And did those feet
               Leave in a huff?
Celia I think they did.
Chris (*singing*) As they have left so
               Oft be-fore.
Ruth (*starting tidying*) Oh I feel terrible.
Jessie (*helping her*) Don't worry, Ruth. It's nothing a little harvest punch won't cure.
Cora Yeah well what time's it turning up?
Chris Come on, let's get this party started!
Cora I need about four gallons after the day I've had.
Annie Let's get it *STARTED*!
Celia Don't tell me you've had another bust up with Ruby?
Cora I think I've had the LAST bust up with my darling daughter for quite a long time, Ceel. (*Beat*) She has disappeared into Europe with some of her mates.
Annie What?
Ruth Ruby's *run away*?
John (*off*) Ladies of the WI!
Cora THE GODS BE PRAISED. IT'S MISTER PUNCH!

John Clarke (Annie's husband) appears, carrying quite a large glass flagon of home brew

After twenty-eight years of marriage, John's appearance still makes Annie smile

Chris LADIES AND GENTLEMEN, MISTER JOHN CLARKE IS IN THE HOUSE.

Cora does a piano flourish

John Who's upset Marie?
Chris Well I think you should ask your wife that. She has behaved DESPICABLY. She deliberately sabotaged the projector so we never got to see the end of "From Russia With Broccoli".

Celia I have to say your man's looking VERY chiselled these days. (*To John*) Not got you on a health kick, has she?

Annie and Chris make eye contact

Ruth My Eddie's joined a gym, did I tell you? For bodytone? Goes three times a week.

John presents his lethal brew

John Ladies! This year's vintage. "John Clarke's Knapeley Knee-trembler."
Jessie (*with a slight frown*) Actually John, Celia's right you know? You *have* lost weight. Your *cheeks* are really/ looking —
Chris (*leaping in*) God I wish y'd have a word with my Rod. He's getting a right old paunch.
Annie (*putting her arms round John*) Works too hard, that's his problem.
Chris Well Rod does that. In fact it's gonna get worse. You've heard they're opening a new Tesco up on Craven Park?
Celia I know! Isn't it great! (*In ecstasy*) This town is finally getting a deli!
Chris It's going to be selling flowers, you traitor. That's the LAST thing our shop needs.
Cora WHY ARE WE NOT DRINKING?
John INDEED! Get your glasses, get your glasses ...

John, Celia, Cora, Jessie and Ruth go to the piano with some shot glasses. Annie scoops Chris to a moment of privacy

Annie Thanks for that.
Chris No, really. He does look good, I wasn't just saying.
Annie Yes. Well.

Chris touches at Annie's hair, like she probably did when they were in their twenties

Chris When's he due in the doctor's?
Annie We go on Friday.

The notion of "fingers being crossed" is in the air between these two old mates

John (*calling*) Chris, where's me final ingredient?

Chris (*producing a small paper bag with a fanfare*) Da da da DA-A!
John Oh hey he's a good lad, your fella.
Chris (*holding them up*) Now then. Rod and I give you these sunflower
   seeds from our flower shop on ONE condition. That you, John Clarke,
   come back to this hall and give us a TALK!

Everyone erupts in agreement. John looks round incredulous

John Me?
Chris Spare us from another "history of broccoli" ——
John Do a talk? What've I ever done except work in the dales?
Chris (*going to "throw" the seeds*) Suit yourself.
John All right, ALL RIGHT! (*Rescuing the seeds from Chris*) This is
   me *pièce de résistance*! (*Getting some seeds out*) You take some of
   these ... (*sprinkling them*) ... little parcels of sunlight. Then get one
   of these —— (*he takes a gas candle-lighter pen from his pocket and
   clicks it*)
Celia Good God.
John Set fire to the top, toast the seeds — turns your mouth into liquid
   Yorkshire!
Ruth Oh I've had one of these! My Eddie did some last Christmas. Set
   fire to the decking.
Jessie In light of which, might I suggest we attempt this outside.
Chris Everyone out!
Cora (*grabbing the drink with zeal*) I'm gone, honey, I am already gone.

Chris, Cora, Celia, Jessie and Ruth bustle out

John swings Annie back

John Come here, you. (*He kisses her*)
Annie How was your day?
John Thrill me. Tell me something I didn't know about broccoli.
Annie Put it this way. I now know as much about broccoli as Chris
   knows about t'ai chi.

John laughs

   (*Over this*) The only difference is, I don't try to teach a class on it.
John Hey. Don't knock it. (*He strokes her hair*) Thirty years ago if
   that woman hadn't fallen off a table trying to get a whole Chinese
   restaurant singing *Jumping Jack Flash*, you and I would never have
   met. (*He holds her face as if recalling this moment — possibly more*

heavily than he might normally do) I only plucked up courage to ask you to the cinema 'cause I was picking noodles out of your hair.
Annie (*after a beat, stroking his hair back*) You were up Grizedale?
John I was. Overseeing junior rangers putting up forest fences. God, they all look about twelve.
Annie I know.
John (*after a beat*) Then this afternoon I nipped in to see ol' Doc Morton.
Annie (*instantly turning to ice*) Today?
John Now don't —— (*"get het up"*)
Annie I thought you wanted me with you.
John Mrs Clarke. There isn't a day goes by when I don't. (*Beat*) I just kind of needed to get the results on me own.
Annie So what did it ...? The blood, the cells, what was it in the end? They think it's OK. (*Telling him the answer she wants to hear*) Fixable. With blood. It's just — transfusion, isn't it? Did he say ...? What er — what it'll take?

Chris appears in the doorway

Chris JOHN! You'd better get out here! Cora's on fire.
John (*smiling*) Oh God.

John heads out, passing Chris who clings to the door frame in ecstasy

Chris (*as John passes*) That — is one hell of a brew. (*Pointing*) They've only had one glass — Celia's dancing on her Porsche, Jessie's picking a fight with a "keep left" sign ... (*She knows in a micro-second something's wrong*) What's the matter?
Annie (*beat, then on autopilot*) I'm fine.
Chris I have not put up with you for four hundred years to be batted off with an "I'm fine".

Annie takes her time

Annie John's got his results.

Chris doesn't have to ask further. After twenty-nine years "putting up", she doesn't need telling. She just goes to her oldest friend and holds her

Chris guides Annie out

Music starts to play: "We Plough the Fields and Scatter"

SCENE 2

The church hall. Winter

The music mutates into "God Rest Ye Merry, Gentlemen"

Marie enters, dressed like something out of Dickens, carrying a candle lamp on a stick, shoulders covered in snow

Marie Come on, Cora *please.*

No one's in the hall

Well where is everyone? *Cora!*

Cora skulks in with a 1970s torch half-heartedly taped to an old golf club

Cora Yo ho sodding ho.
Marie Did you hear High Ghyll? D'you see what I mean now? THAT is why they've been asked to perform the opening *Jerusalem* at National Conference.

Jessie enters with her "lantern", also covered in snow

Right. I need to check this flat-bed truck Chris has organized. (*Heading out of the door*) You two start running through the song.

Marie exits

Jessie May I just ask whose idea was this fake snow?
Cora Whose d'you think?
Jessie It's already gone down the flappy bit round my gearstick and I know damn well it'll still be there come July.

Ruth enters with a fake handbell also like something out of Dickens

Ruth Oyez! Oyez! Oh I think it's a nice little touch of Marie's, don't you? All this with the Victorian — you know — kind of "Dickens" — *Oyez!* (*She clangs her bell*)

A long-coated Celia comes in looking very chic with matching ear muffs and designer shades. And a hangover

Celia I warn you now, Little Dorrit — one more dong out of that and you are both going in the river.

Cora Did you hear High Ghyll's *God Rest Ye Merry*? They sound like the sodding Vienna bloody Boys' Choir.

Celia I have to say you wouldn't know you were brought up in a vicarage.

Ruth Marie said her Jenny sang that version with the Cheshire School Choir at Tatton Hall.

Cora Did she. Well my Ruby sang this version last Christmas Eve in the Ram's Head. (*Singing, to the tune of "Blueberry Hill"*)
            O little town — do do dooody do
            (*Waving them all to copy*) Of Bethlehem — do do ——
     (*Speaking*) Come on
                    — doody doo

Ruth ⎫
Jessie ⎬ (*variously starting to join in*) How still we see — Doo doo
Celia ⎭   doody doo...

Marie races in

Marie Cora!

Cora (*curtsying*) Hello.

Marie What's this?

Cora The song. You wanted a song for the float.

Marie A *carol*, I wanted, Cora. For *Christmas*! For a float that's going to be in full view of *Lord and Lady Cravenshire* ——

Cora Marie, I am sorry I can't offer you a twenty-eight part harmony but High Ghyll have got Enid Richmond who runs Ripon Cathedral bloody Choir.

Marie (*gesturing to her dress*) I know that! THAT'S why I compensated with the Victorian theme. THAT'S why we need something with a little Victorian decorum.

Chris enters and whips off her coat to reveal a Santa baby doll outfit

Chris Well hell — o, Santa!

Marie (*pointing*) NO.

Chris What?

Marie NO, Chris, ABSOLUTELY not. This is a VICTORIAN ——

Rod bursts in

Rod OK! EVERYONE IN THE BACK OF THE VAN!

Marie The "VAN"?

Annie enters with a Victorian lantern

Annie Good GOD Almighty.
Marie NO! Rod! Hold on — (*Pointing accusingly at Chris*) Your wife clearly promised me a flat-bed "*truck*".

Marie races out, past Rod

Rod (*following*) What?

Rod exits

Annie That's never the outfit you bought for our Millennium party?
Chris And I'm still in it, babe. I am STILL IN IT!
John (*off; singing*) Deck the halls with boughs of ——

John enters, dressed as Santa

The girls give him a warm welcome

YO ho ho — oh NOW then! (*Indicating Chris*) THAT is what I call a stocking filler.
Annie (*hitting him*) D'you mind?
John (*to Chris*) Have you been a good little girl this year?
Chris I have, Santa.
John Oh that's a shame.
Annie You'll scare the children.
John Eh I can do that already. (*He removes his hat to reveal a head bald through chemotherapy. Spookily*) Wooo ...

Annie drags the hat back on

Annie It's not scary at all. I actually think it's quite sexy.
Chris (*to Celia*) Hey, nice coat, Ceel. Very demure. D'you want to start a book on who gets most coins in her bucket?
Celia Oh Chris, Chris, Chris. Collecting money has nothing to do with your dress. It's about the rapport you build up with the public using the spirit of your character.

She removes her coat to reveal she has an even shorter Santa baby doll than Chris's

I mean the outfit HELPS, but ——
Chris (*pointing*) NO. That is NOT FAIR.
John D'you know what? I *love* Christmas.

Rod bursts back in

Rod Someone stop me before I kill that woman. God help me, I only
have gladioli but I will find a way ——

Marie careers in

Marie (*wailing*) CHRIS ...!
Rod (*mimicking the intonation, as a "stop me" to John*) JOH-HN...!
Marie You promised me a "truck" and that is in NO sense oh ——
(*seeing Celia*) — oh for GOD'S *SAKE.*
John WHOA whoa whoa ...!

Frenzy all calms

We'll be fine. We'll walk and sing.
Annie We can't do that.
John 'Course we can. Long history, isn't there, Cor? (*Putting his arm
around Cora*) New Orleans? Jazz and religion?
Cora Oh god, our band at college — that's all we did, me and Ruby's
dad. Gospel,/ blues ——
John "Gospel"! There you go! We'll be "The Knapeley Rhythm and
Blues Choir"!
Annie We can't.
Marie We don't have much CHOICE/ Annie ——
Annie John *can't walk that far.*

This creates a hole in the room

John Ohh God that's it. I knew it'd happen. I've turned into the third
person.
Marie (*remembering*) Right. Sorry. (*Beat*) How's the —— ?
John My treatment's going fine, love. And you know what cheers me
up? That WI calendar with your lovely photos of Yorkshire churches.
(*Putting his arm round Marie*) Being able to mark my chemotherapy
appointments under images of misty graveyards.

Chris really smiles. Even Annie does

John Serious. I'd taken it in and one of the guys at the hospital, porter, Lawrence, great lad, *great* photographer — (*to Annie*) *God* you should see some of the ones he's done of his parents ——
Annie (*smiling*) Finish your story.
John (*nodding at Marie*) About your calendar. *Very* complimentary.
Marie Really?
John (*putting his arm out*) Lead on, my little elf. (*For Annie's benefit, wryly*) Remember "he" can't walk that fast.

Marie can't do anything but lead him out

The others follow

Rod (*privately, to Annie*) One day, tell your husband he prevented the world's first gladioli homicide.
John (*off, calling back*) Hey are we jingling or not?
Cora Two three ... (*Singing*) JINGLE BELLS! JINGLE BELLS ...
Celia
Cora
Jessie   } (*leaving; singing together*) Jingle all the way!
Rod   Oh what fun it is to ride
               In a one horse open sleigh ...
    Celia, Cora, Jessie and Rod exit

Chris turns back to her oldest friend and knows what's going on in there

Chris How does he do it? How did such a beautiful man end up with an old git like you?

Annie manages a smile

Annie He'll freeze. Where's that blanket Ruth knitted for Africa and they sent back?
Chris (*"I'll get it"*) How was today?
Annie Fine. Long as it's not septicaemia, we're always fine.
Chris Right. That's ...?
Annie Septicaemia means the chemo stops working. (*Beat*) Mind you it's me who's gonna get septic off that bloody settee in the relatives' room.
Chris Oh God thank GOD you've said that. I thought it was just me putting on weight. It's lethal isn't it? Bloody prongs ... They're gonna need another wing soon, for relatives of people who got injured in the bloody relatives' room.

There's a car horn outside

Chris Did I ever show you where it scratched me?
Annie (*re. Chris's dress*) No, love. But one gust of wind tonight —
Chris Get OFF!

They fall into the usual banter and scrapping. Music starts to "Jingle Bells!"

Annie and Chris tumble out

The random jingling of Christmas bells sharpens to the synchronized jingling of morris dancer bells

SCENE 3

The church hall. Spring

The seasons have passed. Christmas has given way to spring

Jessie enters with flowers and a half-hearted "basket". She starts to arrange them

Jessie No, I'm sorry, Ruth, I know it's a very sad state of affairs but I have come to dread this Spring Fête, I REALLY have.

Ruth bounds in, all excited in a costume — passionately homemade — of a brown animal. The ears hang down round her face

Ruth Oh come on, Jess, it's fantastic, having it on home soil! It's *always* up at High Ghyll! AND we've got a full turnout! Annie's baking one of her cakes, Cora's doing "Tea Tray Decorated on an International Theme"...
Jessie Precisely. The events are completely ridiculous. I mean for a kick off — and I know you don't like bad language but you are dressed as a bloody mouse!
Ruth I'm a rabbit. I was up all night making this. I just need some coathangers to keep me ears up. (*She goes to look in the mirror*) What's your event?
Jessie (*bitterly*) "Arrangement of Flowers Inspired by a Song". Shoot me now.
Ruth I think Marie in fairness just wanted to make sure we had an entry in each category because —
Jessie Because she's *toadying*, Ruth. Because the judge is Lady Cravenshire. She's got me decorating baskets for a landowner's wife.

Now if that makes you feel good, fine, but it makes *me* feel like a
bloody feudal peasant.
Ruth Jessie.
Jessie Sorry.

Jessie tips the basket upside down so all the flowers fall out

Ruth Well what song's that?
Jessie "Where Have All The Flowers Gone?"

Jessie exits

*Chris comes in with a tray of bottled beers which seems also to feature
a small green-flamed candle*

Chris Rod? Is he in...? Rod? G-argh! I will KILL him. I told my husband
QUITE clearly, "Take cake tin to church hall. Do not pass beer tent.
Do not LOOK in beer tent —— " (*nodding perfunctorily*) Sorry, Ruth.
Well done on the ferret.
Ruth I'm not a fer —— Argh. (*Seizing the tray*) That's Cora's "Tea Tray
On An International Theme".
Chris Is it? I wondered what the cotton reels were.
Ruth They're palm trees. The cotton reels are palm trees and the Ferrero
Rocher wrappers are "the golden waves of Montego Bay." (*She bends
the green "palm leaves" back into position*)
Chris (*staring at Ruth*) You know if more people did WI there'd be half
the need for hallucinogenic drugs.

Rod appears with a cake tin, having had a couple of beers

Rod HA HEYY! Has anyone ever told you you're the most byyyoootiful
wife a man could ever have? (*He hugs Chris*)
Chris (*smiling as he hugs her*) Yes. You, every time y've had more than
two pints. Give!
Rod Are you aware that Marie is walking round in a hat the size of a
NASA satellite dish?
Chris She'll be tracking Lady Cravenshire. Any money, by now Marie
will have started speaking like she's at the Cheshire Polo Club.
Ruth How are we doing out there?
Rod The latest results from Knapeley Spring Fête. (*Into a beer bottle
microphone*) High Ghyll have scored five point sevens in the baking
with a display of synchronized flapjacks. West Hebden however have
been disqualified from Garden Produce after their winning courgette
was found to have been born a cucumber.

Chris (*turning him one-eighty*) Y'know what, go back to your beer tent.
Rod Final results from the lemon curd are delayed until the judge has finished being sick —
Chris Look, don't — (*"take the mickey"*) I am only here at ALL 'cause of you, Rod Harper. I only joined the WI to make your mother think I was respectable.
Rod Didn't work.
Chris (*pointing*) OUT.

Rod scuttles out

I hope you're keeping an eye on your Eddie in that tent.
Ruth Oh no, no. He's at the gym. Craven Health Spa. Pumping iron.
Chris The Craven Spa? God. That's a bit pricey.
Ruth Well it's the equipment, Chris. Like he says, you pay for the quality of the aerobic equipment.
Chris He should be here. With you. (*Beat — how to say this...?*) Ruth, he's not playing around again is he?

Instant deflector shields go up

Ruth This isn't your event. Wasn't *Annie* down for the baking?
Chris Annie has currently got more on her plate than cakes.
Ruth Oh, but still she won't forget. Normally Annie is the/ one who NEVER —
Chris Ruth, she's spent the last three months on the A59 running John in and out of Skipton Hospital. "Normally" has gone out of the window.

Annie bursts in, panting, carrying a basket

Annie CHRIS-S! THE CAKE! OH MY GOD! THE *STALL* — OUR *ENTRY* — I WAS SUPPOSED TO BAKE A CAKE!
Chris (*to Ruth*) Told you.
Annie I GOT OUT OF THE CAR AND THOUGHT, "I WAS SUPPOSED TO DO SOMETHING FOR TODAY"/ AND I —
Ruth It's all right. Chris has saved the day.
Chris Ta-da!

Beat

Annie You *baked* something?
Chris Look, I'm not a total dead loss as a woman you know. I can't knit or make plum jam but I can bake a bloody Victoria sponge.
Annie All right, all right. (*She hugs Chris in gratitude*) Thank you.

Chris I mean I haven't baked THIS one, like. I got it from Marks and
  Spencers, but in PRINCIPLE ——
Annie (*trying to get it off her*) WHAT?
Ruth MARKS AND SPENCERS?
Chris We have to enter something for the points.

There is a tussle over the illegitimate sponge

Annie You can't enter a bought cake!

Celia pushes in John in a wheelchair. They both have bottles of beer

Chris Why not?
Celia BEEP BEEEP.
Annie I am not entering a BOUGHT CAKE.
Chris Right. Then *I* will. Make way for my glorious cake.

Chris exits

Celia I think he's putting on a bit of weight, your fella.
Annie Absolutely he is. He's not allowed beer though, Celia.
Celia Oops. (*She takes it off John*) Marie's fault. She should never have
  put me in charge of a putting competition. My mind turns to alcohol
  as soon as I get near a golf bag.
Ruth Why d'you play it, then?
Celia Because otherwise I'd never get to see my husband, Ruth. And I
  quite enjoy the "golf". It's just the bags I have to play it with. (*As she
  swigs beer*) Come on.
Ruth Oh I can't, Ceel. I can't play golf.
Celia I don't want you to play. I want the kids to think you're one of the
  prizes. (*Ushering her out*) "Get a hole in one, win a gerbil."
Ruth For the last time, I'M A RABBIT!

Celia and Ruth exit

*Suddenly it's just Annie and John. Her heart could break seeing him in
that wheelchair*

Annie (*taking a carton of fruit juice from her basket and wielding it
  at John*) Vit-a-mins. (*She sits by him and gives him a drink*) And you
  mustn't get cold. (*She takes a rug from her basket and puts it on his
  knee*) How's it going out there?

*John's breath is shorter than before. Every sentence requires
recuperation*

John　In an extraordinary upturn of events ... (*Pause*) ... I won the Fell
Race. (*A beat*) Wasn't so good going UP hill. (*Pause*) But I came
down in eight seconds.

John has always made Annie laugh

Annie　D'you think you could manage a scone? I hear High Ghyll's are
hotly tipped.
John　(*winking*) Pocket.
Annie　What about it?
John　Present.
Annie　For me?
John　(*his breath is short*) I'd get it meself — suddenly feels such a
bloody distance.

Annie pulls out a white paper bag from John's pocket

Annie　So it's not a diamond necklace then.
John　Better. Much better. (*He smiles*) Sunflower seeds. Plant out round
May. (*Beat*) Up on the hill. (*Beat*) Then call Lawrence. I've promised
he could photograph 'em.
Annie　(*rallying a little*) You are talking, John Clarke, like YOU won't
be doing any of this. And I can tell you, mate, you're down to do a talk
at the WI. And there's certain promises on this mortal coil that cannot
be broken.
John　On the bag. (*He nods*) Started writing it.

Annie looks. The packet has writing on

As I think I said in the Odeon Cinema in Buttermarket Street when all this
began — (*pause*) — if you want a snog you'll have to come to my seat.

Only when Annie tries NOT to, do we realize she's crying

Annie　I think you'll find it was me who said that, John Clarke. And it
was you who very much came scuttling over to MY seat. (*She goes
to hug him*)

Ruth enters, followed by Celia, to move the piano

Ruth Quick, quick she's coming, she's coming.
Celia Calm down, Ruth, or you're going to have a kitten.

Rod enters. Jessie follows. Rod toots on his beer bottle

Rod Ladiee-es and gentlemen ...
Jessie (*at the cuddling couple*) Hey. None of that. We are in the presence of greatness.

The slightly supercilious figure of Lady Cravenshire enters, followed by Marie, as predicted in posh-voice mode. Chris and Cora follow on

Lady Cravenshire Oh now this is *certainly* Victorian ...
Marie   ... absolutely it is, I think you're absolutely right, Lady Cravenshire.
Lady Cravenshire I mean the main church building certainly has the *feel* of Victoria ...
Marie Well Cora will know. Her father used to be vicar here. Cora what is the church?
Cora (*for the benefit of the girls*) In my experience? Intransigent and hypocritical.
Marie (*moving swiftly on*) Thank you so much. And this is Celia, who's only recently joined us!
Celia Yes! Actually at this fête last year, in fact!
Cora She defected from the old bags of the Royal Yorkshire Golf Club.
Marie Of which Lady Cravenshire is Chairman. So anyway, that's wonderful. Lady Cravenshire please ... (*gesturing "do go on"*) ... Do er ...
Lady Cravenshire Ladies. Thank you so much for inviting me to be part of your Spring Fête. I do LOVE coming down this part of the dale.
Jessie (*mock-doffing a cap*) And we loves 'avin' you, ma'am.
Lady Cravenshire As ever it's inspiring to see the amount of enthusiasm on display in all disciplines, especially by those in the "fancy dress" competition, which of course this year is on a theme of "Cowboys and Indians".

Everyone looks at Ruth. She surreptitiously slides her headgear off. Some girls pat her on the back by way of condolence

Some of the baking categories have been judged and I'm pleased to announce that the winner of this year's May Wilkinson trophy for Victoria sponge maximum twelve inch diameter is Knapeley entry two-one-three.

An ecstatic Marie leads the applause, and the other girls follow. The horror dawns. People look at each other

Chris doesn't take this in at first, until Cora and Celia look at her in horror

Chris (*sotto voce*) Help me-ee ...
Annie (*through her fingers*) Oh my Godd-d.
Ruth Oh now *that's* interesting.
Jessie (*putting her hand up*) Over here!
Celia Nice knowing you, Chris.
Cora (*sotto voce*) Come on, Chris. This way through. Dead man walking.

Chris goes up to Lady Cravenshire over the applause. Lady Cravenshire gives her a trophy

Chris (*trying to skulk off as quickly as possible*) Right. Thanks. That's very ——
Lady Cravenshire And I'm ALSO proud to announce ...

Chris stops dead in horror

... that this cake also wins the overall ...
Annie Oh no ...
Lady Cravenshire (*producing a blue sash*) ... Lady Cravenshire Discretionary Award!

Everyone applauds. A proud Marie drapes the sash over Chris

Listen, I never normally ask this, but the *lightness* of that sponge ... is there a thing, a technique how you got that?

Annie turns away, unable to look

Chris Well erm ...
Annie (*sotto voce*) Don't try-y ...

It suddenly dawns on Chris that any spotlight is a spotlight

Chris I basically stuck to my mother's advice about cake baking.
Lady Cravenshire (*nodding, sagely*) Yes-s.
Chris Line the bowl with butter. (*Beat*) Always use a warm spoon. (*Beat*) And if it's a special event, get it from Marks and Spencers.

Silence. Lady Cravenshire is the first to laugh. Then Marie, out of naked relief

Music plays

The laughter ripples back until everyone is laughing and clapping. The unfettered camaraderie unique to a group of women together. Amid this Chris curtsies. On stage. A little bit of a star

We move to a time outside the seasons, a space between hall and dale. Annie wheels John to a position where he reads his speech to the girls, off the paper bag which contains the sunflower seeds

John   (*reading*) "The flowers of Yorkshire are like the women of Yorkshire. Every stage of their growth has its own beauty.

The women listen

   "But the last phase is always the most glorious.

Seeing what we're seeing, we'd have to agree

   "Then, very quickly, they all go to seed.

There is gentle laughter amongst the women in the room

   "Which makes it ..."

   He stops. He gets up out of his wheelchair and puts the speech down where he sat. And walks out through the girls

The girls don't notice. They keep looking at the wheelchair where he once was

Annie goes over to the wheelchair and picks up the bag to read

Annie   (*reading*) "...Which makes it ironic my favourite flower isn't indigenous to the British Isles, let alone Yorkshire. I don't think ..."

She can't. She passes it to Chris

Chris   (*reading*) "I don't think there's anything on this planet that more trumpets life than the sunflower. For me, that's because of the reason behind its name. Not because —— "

It's Chris's turn now to find it impossible to continue

As if in understanding at this, John's own voice (recorded or from a microphone offstage) takes over, in the air above the dales

It is those dales which now appear, as the scene change takes place as he speaks

John's voice "Not because it 'looks like' the sun. Because it *follows* the sun. During the course of the day, the head tracks the journey of the sun across the sky. A satellite dish for sunshine. Sow these seeds on the hill and you'll see ...

Chris passes the bag round and the girls sow the sunflower seeds. Annie lays John's rug on the ground

... that wherever light is, no matter how weak, these flowers will find it. Which is such an admirable thing. (*Beat*) And such a lesson in life."

SCENE 4

John's hill. Early summer

Birdsong. We are high above the River Wharfe, in Yorkshire's green and pleasant land

Chris, Celia, Ruth, Jessie and Cora are all staring up, slightly wincing into the sunlight, with their own thoughts. At the front, Chris goes to Annie

Chris Are we gonna do this, then? You want to do the talking?
Annie (*smiling gently*) I'll be your glamorous assistant.

Chris gives her a squeeze

Chris RIGHT. Let's get going!

They all start doing the "Heaven And Earth" t'ai chi move

Cora OK so remind me — do we milk the yak or shoot it?
Chris No no no forget the t'ai chi. Jessie, pass me that bag?
Jessie (*giving Chris a plastic bag*) I thought you were boycotting that new supermarket because of its low-priced imported flower policy.
Chris I was. But that supermarket also happens to ...

Celia gets out a fold-out microstool and perches on it

... Ceel, what're you doing?
Celia Just 'cause I moved to Yorkshire doesn't mean I have to sit on it. (*Of her trousers*) These are Gina Pellegrini.
Chris (*raising her eyes to heaven, continuing*) That supermarket happens to have a key-cutting and engraving booth which I needed-d — for THIS. (*To Annie*) Exhibit A.

Annie takes a shiny gold plaque from the bag and hands it to Chris, which she passes to the girls

Ruth (*reading from the plaque*) "The John Clarke Memorial Settee."
Chris Which will be placed directly above the settee which thanks to US will be replacing the man-eating settee currently in the cancer wing of Skipton General. Exhibit B.

She nods to Annie who takes a ripped-out page of a catalogue from the bag and hands it round

Annie It's number six.
Chris What d'you think about THAT settee?
Jessie (*taking it*) Oh now.
Cora I think that is probably the settee that God has.
Chris But then I thought, "Hmm. Likely proceeds from next year's calendar?" Marie's "Bridges of Wharfedale"? All I'll say is remember the look on the face of that RSPCA bloke when we handed over last year's cheque? Kind of: (*frowning*) "Cheers girls, that'll just about pay for a hamster's leg splint".
Jessie So ...?
Chris "So" what did Celia discover in the market square at Christmas? Flesh sells.

Annie takes a selection of calendars from the bag and hands them out to them all

My glamorous assistant will give you now, OK, a selection of calendars.
Annie Statistically according to Roy in the post office all of these last year raised more money than "Views Of Local Churches".

There is a pause. They all look at what they're holding

Annie and Chris stand back together to gauge the group reaction

Jessie What's yours got on, Cora?
Cora Not a lot, Jessie.
Celia I have to say I find it difficult to believe that she could ride a motorbike wearing that. (*Beat*) And if she did, it wouldn't stay on very long.
Ruth Well I have to say, I don't mind doing this.

They all turn to look at her with some surprise

I mean it's not — you know, NORMALLY my kind of thing, but if it raises money for a good cause — I don't mind buying one.
Annie Ruth, we're not talking about buying one.
Chris We're talking about *appearing* in one.
Ruth (*shooting up like a rocket*) OH MY GOD.
Chris Calm down.
Ruth Oh for God's SAKE you are JOKING?
Chris (*producing a camera*) Look, the whole point ——
Ruth (*pointing in fear*) OH MY GOD, SHE'S BROUGHT A CAMERA.
I KNEW this wouldn't be about t'ai chi.
Chris We need to raise money quickly ——
Ruth Yes, and with respect anyone else would think "tombola".
Chris RUTH ——
Ruth Maybe "a raffle". There is only YOU on God's EARTH ——
Annie And John.

They all turn to Annie

Who inspired this. Of course. (*She turns the paper bag of seeds, very gently, as evidence. Reading*) "The last phase of the flower is the most glorious."
Chris "The last phase — is the most glorious."
Ruth With respect, Annie, he didn't say "whip your bras off".
Celia Yes, and I'm not a prude. In fact I have in my time ridden *completely* topless on a Harley Davidson but the point is I was sixteen at the time!
Ruth Precisely. (*A beat*) You did *what?*
Chris Ruth! You're making the fatal mistake of confusing "naked" with "nude". Would you call the Venus de Milo "naked"?
Ruth I'm not saying/ that ——
Chris "Being naked" involves detail. "Being nude" involves ... (*She gestures for "le mot juste"*)
Cora Whisky.

Chris Suggestion. What we are talking here is a slight shift from a WI
Calendar of Spectacular Views, to a calendar of ... "Spectacular Views
of the WI."

Chris gives Annie the camera

And today, here on John's Hill, I am about to prove it is possible to
take a photo that celebrates corporeal beauty of the mature human
form without ANY indecency.

*Chris slips her bra out from under her blouse and throws it over her
shoulder*

Are we ready? Ta-da!
Ruth (*catching it in horror*) Oh for God's SAKE.
Jessie You caught it. You're next.
Chris *OK girls. Stand back and prepare for art.* THREE, TWO, ONE.
(*She slings her blouse over her shoulder and turns to look back at the
camera à la "Picture Post"*) Now. Can anyone see my nipples?

The girls are stunned into silence

Suddenly there's a vehicle horn in the near distance

(*Throwing her blouse back on*) Oh my GOD.

*There's a colossal and painful-sounding distant crash. The girls all
run to look. They stand there a few seconds. Then they all turn back to
Chris*

Cora Chris, put your top back on. Girls, I think it's only fair we help
that guy pull his tractor off that wall.

Music plays

*Chris, Cora, Jessie, Ruth and Celia all clear in a state of some
concern*

*Annie picks up the rug they spread on the floor. As she folds it, it unfolds
a private memory*

SCENE 5

The church hall. Later that summer

Lawrence, a slightly shambling young man, enters with a scrabby art folder

Lawrence Annie?

Annie turns and looks at him. There's a beat. It's like she just heard an echo of a voice

It makes Lawrence slightly lose confidence that he's turned up at the right time

("*Are you ok?*") Annie?
Annie Lawrence! Sorry. I was ... (*She folds the blanket*) ... wasn't sure you'd actually ... (*"come"*) You looked a bit stunned in the hospital when we came in to ask.
Lawrence Yeah well. Normally it's a nightmare trying to find a life model. Suddenly a bus load turn up.

Celia, Cora, Ruth and Jessie enter, followed by Chris herding them

Chris IN in in in! Ha! Lawrence. Good lad.

They all pile in. Annie closes the door for privacy

OK. Lawrence! Ladies, this is Lawrence. Porter at Skipton General Hospital.
Annie And a photographer. Proper one.
Celia
Ruth } (*together, with a little wave*) Lawrence.
Cora (*nodding*) All right.
Jessie (*with some recognition*) Hello, Lawrence.
Chris Sorry about all the subterfuge, having to hang around in the car park. It's just it's our president, Marie. She's a bit like that thing out of *Lord of the Rings*, y'know? The big eye — the big ... (*beat*) ... actually she's like quite a FEW things out of *Lord of the Rings* ...
Annie Stop it-t ...
Chris OK. Lawrence, this is Miss January, February, March and April ...

Celia, Cora, Ruth and Jessie all rise up in arms

Celia ⎫   ⎧ Whoa whoa whoa
Jessie ⎬ (*together*) ⎨ Hold on...
Ruth ⎪   ⎪ Annie?
Cora ⎭   ⎩ Hey let's just take things easy ——
Annie (*placating*) IF — if they decide to go ahead. (*She nods*) You said
on the phone you'd had an idea.
Lawrence (*nervous as hell*) Right. Well. When you ——

Chris gestures to him to address the group

    — when they came in the hospital — Chris and Annie — about this
    — this calendar what you're wanting to sell at the Yorkshire Show ...
    what it ... what they er ... (*He swallows*)
Cora Christ, love, if you're intimidated NOW, what are you gonna be
like when Celia takes her blouse off?
Chris *Cora.*
Celia Mesmerized.
Lawrence (*swallowing almost audibly*) It should be what John said.

This quietens them all slightly

    When I was pushing him round. Talking to him about what it was
    you all did in here. He reckoned all the jam-making and knitting was
    basically a front for a load of respectable middle-aged women to get
    together and go nuts.

*There's a beat where the room feels momentarily warmed by John's
humour. It gives Lawrence some confidence*

    That's what your calendar should be.

He gets the drawings out. They all crowd round

    At first glance the photos should look like your classic WI calendar.
    All your traditional ... cakes, jam, sewing an' that. *Everything* y'd
    expect. Except for one tiny thing. The person doing it is naked.
Everyone (*quietly, variously*) Nude.

He shows the first sketch. We don't see it

Pause

Annie You're right. John would've loved this.

Lawrence (*warming to his theme*) See so each month, y'see, y'd get a different girl ... (*he hands out pages*) — painting, knitting, *gardening* here, see ... until December when I thought we could do a group one of you all together singing Christmas carols.

The last sketch is a double spread. It creates a huge reaction

Chris Ohmygod that just ... Lawrence that is PERFECT! We LOVE it! We AB-solutely —
Cora Except for one small problem. (*Beat*) He's a *bloke*.
Jessie I thought the point was we're not actually going to be showing anything.
Cora On the *photographs*. I imagine there's going to be considerably more on display in the actual bloody *room*.
Chris Cora, we've BEEN through this. An artist doesn't see a naked woman, he sees a "life model". (*To Lawrence*) Don't you, Lawrence?

They all look at Lawrence. He loses what bottle he had

Lawrence I think ... (*He swallows*)
Chris Yes?
Lawrence ... I left me bike on a bend.

Lawrence exits

The girls all watch him go

Chris (*to Cora*) Well thank you very much.
Cora Look. I'm sorry, OK, I'm sorry. It's just — Ruby has already got me down as a woman who makes a habit of ... (*waving loosely*) ..."parading herself in front of men."
Celia Why?

Cora bats it off

Annie Cora —
Celia No, come on you've never done anything like this/ before —
Cora (*killing it dead*) *Because I lost touch with her dad, Ceel.* (*Beat*) Because I'm the kind of mother who "loses touch" with the father.
Annie Look no one's parading ANYTHING.
Chris Lawrence would arrange the photos, leave the room, off comes the dressing gown, one of US would click the shutter.

Beat

Annie   (*collecting the drawings*) Look he's done all these, all this thinking about it. At some point we're going to have to commit to giving it a go or not.

The girls all look at each other

Jessie   Well. I think I can fairly quickly state MY position.
Chris   Jessie, look I appreciate for a woman of your —— (*searching for "le mot juste"*)
Jessie   You know, the last time I heard the phrase "a woman of your age" it was my new, young headteacher explaining his reasons why I should retire. The following week I had to take over the school trip halfway up Plover Hill after he collapsed with exhaustion. (*She pulls her coat on*) I have never had a problem with age, my dear. It has only ever had a problem with me. (*She puts her scarf on*) Any teacher who has seen the years pass with lengthening legs and shortening skirts has felt old since she was thirty. And the danger, girls, of age, is what you think age expects of you. Witness my mother, who at the age of sixty considered a day when the postman and the gas man called to be one where she was, quote, "run off her feet". Why? Because the small incidents of life will expand to fill the hours you allot them, and the saddest thing on God's earth is those with the fewest hours left allowing less and less to fill more and more.

She heads for the door

Chris   (*stopping her*) S—sorry, Jessie. Just to clarify —— ?
Jessie   No front bottoms. (*Beat*) I'm in, as long as there's no front bottoms. That's a sight I've reserved for only one man in my life.
Annie   Right. D'you think your husband will mind?
Jessie   Good God, love, it wasn't my husband.

Jessie exits, shutting the door

Celia   (*standing up and applauding*) WAY TO GO, JESS!

Ruth starts to head out

Annie   Ruth?
Ruth   The thing is ... not all of us are Chris-es. (*Beat*) Some of us are Ruths.
Chris   (*gathering her up*) No no no but see that's the *point*, hun. Having the Ruths. It's not like we're doing it because we want to show off fantastic bodies ...

Ruth But *actually* Chris ... (*choosing her words carefully*) In fairness actually there IS a little bit of that, isn't there? You and Celia? And your little ... "Bra-wars". Which is fine, I'm not saying ——
Celia Don't be ashamed, Ruth.
Ruth ... but not all of us used to ride topless on a Harley Davidson.
Celia Can you not make it sound like I was in the circus? I did it once, to spite my mother.
Chris Ruth, show Eddie what he's missing. You're a beautiful wom ——
Ruth (*snapping*) CHRIS, I'll buy one, OK? I'll buy a hundred. (*She heads out*) For John I'll buy a hundred. I'll be proud of you and buy a hundred.

Ruth exits

There is a pause. Annie looks to Chris. Cora tries to slope unnoticed out of the door

Celia (*realizing*) Cora-a ...

Cora stops and turns at the door

Cora Celia, I am a vicar's daughter, a single mother and the church organist.
Annie And?

This sudden summation of her life hits Cora out of left field

Cora And if I'm not gonna get them out now, when am I?
Celia That's my GIRL!

Chris and Annie hug Cora

Cora Lord forgive me. I know not what I bloody do.

Cora exits

Chris Are you all right with this, Ceel? The ladies of the Royal Yorkshire Golf Club are not going to like this.
Celia Believe me. That's why I'm doing it! (*She hugs Chris*) I'll tell David Bailey I'll do July and if things get tough I don't mind spilling over into the Autumn.

Celia exits

Suddenly it's just Chris and Annie again

Chris I think we've got a calendar! You realize we're going to have to bloody do it now. (*A beat*) How about you, Mrs Clarke? Are *you* all right doing this?
Annie (*thinking a beat*) I wasn't actually. Sure. Not until he walked in.
Chris Lawrence?

Annie starts to say something, but seems to think better of it. Then says it anyway

Annie I knew John agreed. (*Beat*) Somehow I knew J —— Oh God this is what happens isn't it? (*She puts her head in her hands*) You start going mad. Start seeing them in other people. Before long you're seeing them in the markings on your toast. Am I going mad? D'you think I'm going mad?

Chris goes to her and holds her

Chris Love. You're about to take your bra off to buy a settee. You're a complete fruitcake.
Annie (*being hugged*) Hey but hold on. What about "the dark Lord Marrie who sees all, Mister Frodo?"
Chris (*squeezing her*) Don't you worry, my little Gollum.
Annie I wasn't being Gollum.
Chris I think I know a way we can get round Marie.

Black-out

SCENE 6

The church hall. Night, a few days later

There's a flash of lightning. Music of evil-doing plays. A full moon rises in the sky

In the half light, and over the music, Lawrence and Rod enter

Lawrence sets up his props and lights for the shoot, ordering Rod and crew members helping with energetic commands. Together they bring on two lights, a camera on a tripod with remote flash attachment, two reflector shields, a WI catering trolley with a sheet as yet concealing many confectionery masterpieces, climaxing in a tower of cherry buns, two balls of wool on knitting needles, a knitted sheet, a shiny backdrop, Santa Claus hats and a variety of Christmas wine, gift and cracker props, and carol sheets

Lawrence Right, let's get this thing set up. Rod. Quick as you can. (*Indicating the piano*) Careful with that, it weighs a ton!
Rod Trolley covered, or —— ?
Lawrence Trolley covered ... exactly as I marked out on the plans ... Leave the main lights off — Rod make sure all cables are out of the way ... don't want any trip hazards ...
Rod Where d'you want —— ?
Lawrence Down there. That's great. (*Indicating the box of Christmas props*) Right. That's you done, Rod. (*To everyone*) Out. Thanks.

Everyone except Lawrence exits

(*When he's happy it's all set up*) Right, ladies. Ready.

Lawrence exits

The music stops

Jessie enters wearing a Jessie-ish bath robe, followed by Cora, dressed in HER style of bath robe — two girls out of their dormitory at midnight who know they're doing wrong

Celia, robed like she's just sashayed off a film set, glides in pulling a golf trolley

Celia produces a bottle of vodka and shot glasses from the trolley, which she sets up on the piano like a bar. She pours vodka into the glasses. Jessie and Cora react with huge relief

Finally Annie and Chris come in, in fits of silent laughter, also in robes; Annie's is a towelling one, Chris's more chic

Chris Ladies. Welcome.

They all down the vodkas in one

Annie Can we just congratulate Cora.
Chris Yes, tonight's decoy was carried out by Lance Corporal Gleave of the Royal Musical Corps.
Cora (*saluting*) I thank you.

Jessie Well done, Cora.
Everyone Well done, Cora!

Celia pours out more vodka. They all drink another shot

Cora I got the keys by convincing Marie I was starting "The Knapeley WI Choral Society".

They all fall about laughing

Chris She's probably out there now, inviting Lady Cravenshire to our first concert.

We can almost HEAR the heartbeats, the procrastination

Girls. Are we ready?

Celia pours out more vodka. They all drink a shot. More procrastination

Everyone Ready.
Chris (*producing some straws*) Who's going to go first?

No volunteers are forthcoming. Annie steps into the firing line

Annie (*taking a long straw*) Can I just say if it *is* me I shall be proud and honoured and more than anything *happy* to —— (*seeing that it's long*) — OH THANK GOD IT'S NOT ME.

Annie passes the bunch of straws to Celia. Celia pulls the short one

Celia Oh my GOD-D! (*She collapses on the piano keys, grabs the whole bottle and swigs*)
Chris (*calling*) MISS SEPTEMBER!
Everyone SEPTEMBER!

Lawrence enters. He pushes forward the WI catering trolley on wheels, under a sheet

Lawrence September! Just like we rehearsed.

Chris, Annie, Cora and Jessie follow Lawrence's instructions

Chris, camera. Annie, light one there. Cora, light two there ... Cora — Jessie, I need light reflector shields. Jessie up ... up ... (*Etc.*)

Celia shakes her hair like a model. She continues this vigorously, as though trying to shake a bird out of it

An entire photo shoot assembles in seconds round her. Lawrence whips the sheet off the trolley to reveal the Babylon of buns

(*Lining up the "set"*) Left, just move — higher. That's it.

The girls follow his instructions

(*After a beat*) Ready. (*He hands the remote camera to Chris*)

Lawrence races out

Chris (*nodding to Annie*) Go.

Annie goes to take Celia's robe off

Celia STOP!

Celia seems suddenly very vulnerable

Chris Good God, Celia, now's not the time to start being coy.
Celia (*sotto voce*) I know, but ... (*She breathes in heavily. Suddenly all her bravado has dissipated*)
Annie Look, none of us are used to standing in front of people naked, love. Not even husbands. God's sake, John didn't see ME naked until the spring of nineteen seventy-nine.

Beat

Cora What happened in the spring of seventy-nine?
Annie There was a lizard in the shower block at Abergele. In fact quite a few people saw me naked that morning.
Lawrence (*off*) HAVE YOU DONE IT?

They look at Celia. She goes to release her robe, and almost in instinctive sympathy, Cora and Jessie screen her with the reflector shields. Celia turns round, her back to us, and releases the robe. This gives Cora a front row view of Celia's front

Cora Good God. (*She nods at Chris to look round*)

Chris surreptitiously sneaks a look at what Cora's looking at

Chris (*calling off*) Lawrence. We're going to need considerably bigger buns.

Celia turns, grabbing two buns to mask her modesty and holding them up like patisserie headlamps

Lawrence (*off*) DON'T TOUCH THE COMPOSITION!
Annie DON'T TOUCH THE COMPOSITION!
Celia I like the buns "up". They cover more.
Chris Lawrence, were the buns "up" or "flat"?
Lawrence (*off*) FLAT!
Annie Flat for her, or flat for us?

Lawrence bursts in out of exasperation

Lawrence DON'T —

The girls all shriek and move to cover Celia

Lawrence reels straight out again

(*Shielding his eyes as he leaves*) Don't — touch — the buns.
Jessie Don't — touch — the buns.
Annie (*to Celia*) Bad girl.
Chris (*doing the same*) Bun-toucher.
Lawrence (*off*) THE SMILE NEEDS TO BE ENIGMATIC.

Celia tries "enigmatic"

Jessie She looks like she's got pelvic floor trouble.
Annie (*calling*) How d'y' mean, "enigmatic"?
Lawrence (*off*) LEFT SIDE OF THE MOUTH A LITTLE UP.

Celia tries this

RIGHT SIDE POSSIBLY SLIGHTLY DOWN.

Celia tries this

THE CENTRAL AREA KIND OF —
Celia OH for GOD'S SAKE, get him in here.
Chris What?
Celia Get him in here!
Chris LAWRENCE!

Lawrence bursts in, matter-of-fact, and commands the camera

Lawrence   Right. Buns THERE. (*He directs the screens*) Reflectors ROUND. (*To Celia*) What's your husband going to say when he sees this?
Celia   (*half smiling*) I don't know.

Lawrence takes the photo. The camera flashes and there's the loud sound of a camera light

Lawrence   THAT was "enigmatic".

Celia beams

You looked beautiful, Celia. July.

They all cheer

Everyone   JULY!
Cora   Oh Christ, that's me.
Lawrence   Annie! Jessie! Reflectors!

Cora swigs from the bottle, heading for the piano

Cora   Right, right. If I'm gonna get my kit off, I'll need to warm this place up a bit.
Jessie   Make sure your fingers are on the right notes for *Jerusalem*.
Cora   I'll be a bit insulted if they're looking at my fingers, Jessie. (*She starts playing. Singing*) "Bring me my bow ..."
Everyone   (*joining in, variously*) "Of burning gold ..."
Cora   STOP! (*To Lawrence*) Other side. OTHER side. (*Beat*) I've got a tattoo.
Chris   WHAT?
Jessie   Hey, check. Has it got a bloke's name on?

Annie goes to check

Cora   (*fending her off*) GET — OFF!
Annie   It's got seven, all crossed out.
Lawrence   CORA?
Cora   Right, come on, girls, cover me.

Jessie and Annie come round with the reflector shields

Celia Ladies of Knapeley Choral Society. Stand by for "Air Without A
   G-String".
Cora READY!

Jessie and Annie pull back the shields to reveal Cora at the piano

Lawrence Just imagine you're on stage in front of a thousand fans.
Celia And you've shagged every single one of them.
Cora *CHEEK*!

*Lawrence takes a photo. There's a flash and accompanying sound, the
photo capturing that moment of attitude from Cora*

The girls applaud loudly

Lawrence All right ladies. January!
Everyone JANUARY!
Lawrence Jessie.
Jessie Oh my God.
Lawrence That's yours.

*Lawrence hands Jessie two balls of wool on knitting needles. She has a
go at all configurations, but it's hard to imagine how these are going to
cover all three areas*

Jessie What am I supposed to do with THIS?
Annie (*patting Jessie on the shoulder*) If I were you, love, I'd start knitting.
Lawrence You look great. There's nothing to be worried about.

Annie and the girls assemble a knitted sheet around Jessie. She gets ready

Jessie You know what's marvellous is that he *still* hasn't realized.
   (*Calling to Lawrence*) So, young Lawrence Sugden! You clearly don't
   recognize your old school teacher with her clothes *on*.
Lawrence Oh my God.
Jessie How about now?

The girls drop the knitted sheet. Jessie's pose is revealed

*Flash! Lawrence takes the photo. There's an accompanying sound. He
spins away, shell-shocked, grabbing the booze, and swigging heavily*

Annie Come on now, Lawrence. You can't drink your way out of fear.
Celia (*to Annie*) You're next.

Annie (*grabbing the drink*) Give me that.
Celia In you go! Go on. (*Shepherding her to the kitchen*) FEBRUARY!
Everyone FEBRUARY!

They steer Annie behind the serving hatch

Lawrence Celia! Cora! Lights!
Cora (*calling*) Hey if *I've* done it, I hope you're totally bloody naked
in there Annie Clarke.
Annie (*off*) That is something only I and a cupboard of teacups will ever
know. READY!

*The girls open the hatch. Annie bobs through behind a huge teapot
and china cup*

One lump or two?

Lawrence takes the photo. Flash and sound of camera!

The girls cheer loudly

Lawrence October!
Everyone OCTOBER!
Chris I've got to get my props!

Chris races off

Jessie Miss October's gone to get her props.
Lawrence OK, well in the meantime — NOVEMBER!
Everyone NOVEMBER!
Lawrence Give us a hand, Cora! Celia! Mrs Raistrick! Lights! We need
this marmalade table right here!

Lawrence and Cora exit and enter with the "marmalade" set

Celia Marmalade-making coming in!

Annie enters, re-robed

Annie Oh God. Lawrence, I totally forgot. There isn't one for marmalade.
November was going to be Ruth, but she wouldn't —

*BANG! The door flies back, nearly knocking Annie and Lawrence over
and revealing Ruth in a long coat*

Music of suspense! No one quite knows why Ruth's here or what she's going to do

   Ruth?

Ruth has clearly had a few and she goes to seize more alcohol. She drinks for about five seconds, looks round, then making moves akin to a burlesque artist, she looks as if she's starting to undo her coat right in front of Lawrence

Celia ⎫
Cora ⎬ (*together*) On the table!
          ⎭

Staggering slightly, Ruth climbs on the table. Celia and Cora lift the sides of the cloth to form an impromptu changing booth

Cora Lawrence! Don't look!
Ruth (*from inside*) I can do this. I can do this. I can do this ... (*She continues, flinging her coat out followed by the rest of her clothing, dressing gown, shoe, shoe, bra*)

The music grows as Ruth flings her clothes out

   Chris enters with her props: two florists' buckets full of orchids

Ruth flings her pants out from behind the cloth

Chris Ruth?

Celia, Cora, Jessie and Annie nod

   You absolute STAR!
Ruth (*behind the sheet*) Ready!

With a music fanfare, Celia and Cora drop the tablecloth screens to reveal Ruth, glorious amidst fruit

   I DID IT!

Lawrence takes the photo. The camera flashes with accompanying sound. The gang all cheer

Ruth re-dresses into her gown

Cora What the hell changed your mind?
Chris Don't tell me. Surprise birthday present for My Eddie?
Jessie My God. All I got *my* husband was a squirrel-feeder.
Annie You realize your Eddie'll never be able to eat marmalade again without a smile on his face.
Lawrence OCTOBER!
Everyone *OCTOBER!*
Lawrence Annie, Cora, backdrop. Mrs Raistrick — lights!
Celia Yeah, sorry you ended up with the — (*yawning as she says it*) "flower arranging" pose, Chris. (*Patting her shoulder*) Wanna put money on who makes the front cover?
Chris Yeah, it *is* a shame. Backdrop!

Annie and Cora hoist up a shiny backdrop behind Chris and her flowers

I had to make do with some garden twine and a few orchids.

Chris throws off her dressing gown to reveal she's naked except for a scattering of red carnations held in place to cover her modesty by near invisible garden twine. It makes her appear like a classical statue, half ancient Greece, half Vegas, totally fab

READY!

Lawrence takes the photo. There's a flash and accompanying sound! Music kicks in — an R&B version of "Jerusalem". All action is now pinned to this track until the end of the scene. The other girls clap, falling about laughing with surprise. Chris has done it again

Lawrence December-r!
Everyone DECEMBER!
Chris CLEAR THE DECKS! THIS IS THE BIG ONE!
Lawrence MUSIC!

Amidst huge clamour and chat, Santa Claus hats and a variety of Christmas wine, gift and cracker props — along with carol sheets —are distributed

Annie Come on! Ladies, CHRISTMAS IS HERE!
Everyone CHRISTMAS.
Cora Girls, we're going over the top!
Celia I think some of us already have!
Lawrence Presents! Hymn sheets! Tinsel! (*Etc. under:*)
Annie HATS!

There is huge hubbub as they ready themselves. Much ad-libbing

Everyone (*ad-libbing*) Keep that bloody tinsel coming/ behind the piano, behind this piano/ More presents please, Santa!/ Are we sharing a hymnsheet?/ You want to be in front?/ NO No no I'm very happy here... (*Etc.*)

Ad-libbing swells until all are ready to go for the big one

Chris LADIES! HAVE WE DECKED THE HALLS?
Everyone YES!
Chris HAVE WE STUFFED THE GOOSE?
Everyone YES!
Chris ARE OUR DING DONGS MERRILY ON HIGH?
Everyone YES! (*They all cheer!*)
Chris In that case I think it's time to ...

The music and clapping build

Everyone (*clapping*) *OFF! OFF! OFF!*
Lawrence THREE!
Cora (*singing to track until end of act*)
                     "In England's green ..."
Everyone (*singing*) "In England's green ..."
Lawrence TWO!
Cora (*singing*) "And pleasant ..."
Everyone (*singing*) "And pleasant ..."
Lawrence ONE!

All the girls as one disrobe. In a nothing-less-than spectacular flourish of tactical arrangement, the wine, presents and opening carol sheets, at the very last second, preserve all modesty. It's fabulous

   Sadly, it's also just as Marie opens the door and spiritedly ushers Lady Cravenshire in to see her new choir

Marie faints dead

Everyone   (*singing*) "... LAND!"

Black-out

CURTAIN

ACT II

Scene 1

The Annual WI conference, London

The stage is in darkness. At the front is a small lectern and a line microphone. On the lectern is a crude traffic-light warning system for letting speakers know when their speeches are over-running

All the girls enter. Ruth, Jessie, Cora and Celia wait in the darkness out of the lectern spot, ready for Scene 2

Over the lights-down we hear a politely dogmatic female voice

Female voice on tannoy Ladies, if you can just take your seats please ... welcome to this afternoon's session of this year's Annual WI Conference. We'll start with the Emergency Motions for general voting. Quite a number of these to get through this afternoon, so please could all proposers keep to the time limit. First is the delegate from Knapeley WI.

A sudden harsh spotlight slices through the darkness

Annie walks with trepidation towards it, into the limelight. The warning light pings to green. She can go

Annie Ladies of the WI.

It echoes "WI ... WI ... WI ..." It freaks her

We of the Knapeley Branch have been asked here to National Conference, to — to — (*she swallows*) explain ... (*she breathes in*) what we're trying to do is a *calendar* ... (*she nods*) A WI ... to sell at the Yorkshire Show. To buy a seat. *Settee*. For the hospital. Skipton Gen ——

There's a buzz. The amber light comes on. It throws Annie completely

General. Which is where John ... (*Beat*) *My* John ...

Annie loses all speech when she says that name. It is still like a bee sting in her mouth. A short buzz for the red light makes her jump. The warning light changes to red

This cues a warrior-like Chris to storm into the spotlight with Annie

Chris HOLD ON. HOLD ON A MINUTE WITH YOUR BLOODY BUZZER. (*She takes the stand*) Sorry but the OTHER delegate for Knapeley's got something to say and she's about to commit heresy. (*Loudly*) I HATE plum jam. I only joined the WI because it made my mother-in-law happy. End of story. (*Counting on her fingers*) I'm crap at cakes, I hate *knitting* — and in fact seeing it's unlikely George Clooney would ever come to Knapeley to give a talk on his collection of slightly-too-small swimming trunks, there seems very little reason for me to STAY in the WI. *Except* — SUDDENLY I want to raise money in memory of a man we all loved. And to do that I'm prepared to take my clothes off on a calendar. (*Beat*) And if you guys don't agree then I'm going to do it without council approval because FRANKLY, guys, some things are bigger than council approval. And FRANKLY if it meant we'd get — (*she gestures a "tiny amount"*) — THAT-T much closer to killing off this shitty, cheating, sly, conniving, silent bloody disease that cancer is then God, I tell y'. I would run round Skipton market smeared in plum jam with a knitted tea cosy on my head singing *Jerusalem.*

There's a sudden snap back to full light

SCENE 2

The church hall. The following day

All the girls are on tenterhooks. A beat of silence

Jessie To which Central Committee replied...?
Annie "The WI does not 'do' nudity."
Jessie (*recoiling*) Sod them. I KNEW they wouldn't.

There's deflation in the room

Annie
Chris } (*together*) "But we DO do charity".

The deflation instantly reverses!

Jessie (*fisting the air*) Bless them. I KNEW they would!

They all erupt in joy

Cora You're *kidding*? They overruled Marie?
Chris (*putting her arm round Annie*) "As long as it's done with decorum." Which unfortunately rules YOU out, Celia ...
Celia (*deadpan*) Oh aha.
Annie We have permission to call it an "*Alternative* WI Calendar".
Chris Which I have to say comes as one hell of a relief, because I've already had them printed!
Annie What?

Chris gets calendars and hands them out

When did you do this?
Chris The day before we went to London. I checked the deadlines. If we'd left it 'til AFTER the decision, we'd've missed the Yorkshire Show anyway.
Annie Wow. And did they donate it, the printers?
Chris No, no. Rod's got a company credit card. I put it down as "stationery".

They all open the calendars with trepidation

Cora Oh my ...
Jessie Ruth!

Hands fly to mouths all around. But there are shivers of pride in what they see

Celia Blimey, Ruth, you scrub up well.
Cora Good God, Jessie, you look like Jane Fonda.
Ruth (*shrieking and pointing*) CORA!
Cora Oh Christ you can see the tattoo.
Jessie What's he done with all the cellulite?
Celia It's still there, love. It's just in shadow.
Jessie Remind me to spend the rest of my life in shadow.
Celia (*searching*) Where's mine ...?
Chris (*pointing*) It's there! September!

There is a pool of quiet as they ALL arrive at September. Unwittingly they all simultaneously lower their calendars

Cora Good God.
Jessie Celia, I can only offer my congratulations.
Cora Prepare for a life on the internet.

There's a car horn outside

Ruth Marie!

Chris looks at her watch

*Ruth, Cora, Celia and Jessie drop their calendars to the floor. Cora
directs everyone to sing*

Ruth   ⎫
Celia   ⎪
Cora   ⎬ (*together, singing*)   "Dear Lord and Father of Mankind
Jessie   ⎭   Forgive our —— "
Annie (*laughing*) It's OK!
Chris It's all right, IT'S OK. IT'S JUST TONY.
Ruth Who?
Annie Bartholomew. *Craven Herald*. Remember?   ˋ
Chris Took some photos when we did that German Cabaret night. I
   phoned him up to see if he remembered me — which thankfully he did
   ...
Annie Surprise, surprise. No one'll EVER forget your Lily Marlene,
   love. Least of all that lamppost.
Chris (*hitting her*) He's going to do a little piece.

There's a knock on the door

   Stick the kettle on, Cora. Break open the emergency Bourbons. This is
   a WI charm offensive.

   Jessie, Cora and Celia exit into the kitchen

Ruth is more hesitant

Chris Come on, Ruth.
Annie What's the matter?
Ruth Nothing, I just — (*entre-nous*) It's just when you start something
   that's only going to be a few photos that a few people are going to
   see ——
Chris No good if it's that, Ruth. Might as well have had "Bridges Of
   Wharfedale".

Annie We need to make sure people notice us, love. This isn't Knapeley Fête anymore. This is the Yorkshire Show. We're up against the Red Arrows.

Chris That's right. We're now competing with Jeff Randall's Tumbling Sheepdogs. (*Holding the door open*) If we're lucky, we'll get one paragraph on page fourteen.

Annie (*holding the other door open*) Believe me, Ruth. It's not going to go any further than that.

Chris and Annie close the doors on themselves and Ruth

Music plays. Instantly we get a volley of radio and TV commentary

American Male Voice Goooood morning Cincinnati and in the Yorkshire region of England a group of women are putting the "tea" into "nudity" ...

This folds under a Japanese female voice in whose burst of gabble we can pick out the words "Yorkshire" and "WI". This folds under ...

English Male Voice ... some women in the Yorkshire village of Knapeley have been raising funds by raising eyebrows ...

This folds under a French voice ...

French Voice ... pour quelques femmes Anglasies il s'agit de 'liberté, egalité, nudité!'*

SCENE 3

The church hall. A few days later

Music stops. Cora enters at speed. She shuts the door and flattens herself against it, panting.

Cora Ho-ly — COW.
Jessie (*off; the other side of the door*) CORA!
Cora Sorry sorry sorry ...

Cora opens the door and helps Jessie struggle in with a large funeral wreath of white carnations spelling "MUM"

Jessie (*shutting it*) Oh Lord. OH my good Lord.

Cora (*panting*) Did you SEE how many vans there were with those satellite-dishy things?
Jessie That is just ri-diculous!

Ruth tumbles through

Ruth They've shut the road! The police have had to shut the ROAD!
Cora Shut the door!
Ruth Where did they all come from?
Cora Quick. Get a buttonhole! (*She starts to pull carnations out of the wreath*)
Ruth Did Chris *really* mean us to pull this apart?
Jessie It's what she said. (*She hands one out*) Here.
Ruth I mean this is somebody's *mother*.
Jessie It *should've* been. Apparently Chris forgot the funeral because of organizing this press conference. Ended up running down the road behind the hearse asking if they still wanted it.
Ruth All the same, to pull it apart ——
Cora Ruth, what else does she do with it? Put an advert in the "Buy and Sell" saying "Does your Mum look a bit peaky?"

Celia and Annie enter carrying a bag of props

Annie ... no, not her. The one NEXT to the French girl. That guy was definitely speaking Japanese.
Cora (*horror-stricken*) Hold on, what's French? There's not *French* papers?
Celia God Cor, and the rest! American ——
Annie Japanese ——
Cora No no no but seriously? *French*?
Annie What's so bad about France?
Cora Oh for — it's only where Ruby's run off to, isn't it? And now she's gonna see this in some bloody God-knows-where French town, where I'm not going to be THERE to EXPLAIN and oh my God I'm sorry, Ruth, I'm sorry, but ... *bollocks*.
Jessie Sorry Ruth.

Ruth's first instinct is to comfort Cora

Ruth (*rubbing Cora's shoulders*) It's fine. She's fine.
Cora I'm not. I'm a bloody disgrace to motherhood. I'm surprised Marie hasn't volunteered me to do a talk on "How To Rear The Perfect Daughter".

Chris bursts in, buzzing

Chris OH MY GOD this is what I call a press turnout! How're we doing with the buttonholes? (*Clapping, like Marie once did*) Come on, guys, we need to look co-ordinated. (*Starting to organize this*) Just 'cause the press turn up doesn't mean the papers use the photos. That's not how it all works. Can we remember the pose? Jessie? Left foot forwards, right arm back. Smile.

They all do, sort of, and strike it — some (Jessie in particular) with a degree of reluctance

That's my girls! Get your props! Come on, Jess. We're going to do this like we mean it. (*She gives the girls the bag of props*)

The girls dole the props out

Annie It wasn't a problem, was it?
Chris What?
Annie For the business? Forgetting that funeral?

Chris is handed a small corsage

Chris Hey THIS is the business in hand, love. The shop can stand losing a few chrysanths.

Annie is handed a teacup

Annie (*indicating Chris's corsage*) Should be sunflowers.
Chris Believe me if I get this all working, we'll have bloody Amazonian orchids. (*She hugs Annie*) This is our baby. Remember that. All that out there only happened because of you and me.
Annie And John.
Chris Obviously. OK. Stand by. Cora. Ruth. You're up first.
Ruth NO! Not first!
Chris Too late, Ruth! We know you can do it now.
Ruth You said I'd only have to do it once!
Chris (*through the megaphone*) Ladies and gentlemen! From the Knapeley Women's Institute Alternative Calendar ... (*To Ruth*) Come on, Ruth. Show them what you've got! You're STRONG! You're PROUD!
Ruth I'M NOT DRUNK.
Chris (*through the megaphone*) MISS NOVEMBER!

Ruth poses. Flashguns

Ruth goes off

Chris pushes Annie into position

Chris Annie. Pose! Make sure you get your teacup high!
Annie At my age, this is as high as my teacups go.
Chris (*through the megaphone*) MISS FEBRUARY!

Annie poses. Flashgun

Annie goes off

Chris ushers the next ...

Jessie (*to Cora*) Come on. Here's your music, Miss Jerusalem. In
for a penny. (*She grabs Cora, sister-in-arms*) We will show them
our countenance divine. Face it, they've already seen our pleasant
pastures.
Cora (*to the skies*) Ruby, wherever you are, this is your mother. *Je ne
regrette rien.*
Chris (*through the megaphone*) MISS JULY AND MISS JANUARY!

Jessie and Cora pose. Flashgun

Jessie and Cora exit

Celia, you're up next.
Celia (*putting her buns back*) Little experiment. Let's see if EVERYONE
needs props to get recognized.
Chris (*through the megaphone*) MISS SEPTEMBER!

Celia catwalks out with natural aplomb. Several flashes!

Celia Thought not.
Chris (*quietly through megaphone*) I hate you.

Celia exits

(*Loudly through megaphone*) AND FINALLY, MISS OCTOBER!

*Chris stows the megaphone, looks at her rather paltry prop flowers ...
then notices the "MUM" wreath. In a moment of inspiration she grabs
it, jams the flowers in the top of the "U", steps out for the cameras and
gently turns it so it reads "WOW"*

A colossal volley of flashes goes off

Wow!

Chris goes out. She is the only one who doesn't do "the" pose, having taught all the others to. But then Chris is always different from the others

Black-out

SCENE 4

The church hall. A few days later

Functional, unglamorous overhead striplights come on. Marie enters looking super-flash in her super-white badminton kit (John Lewis branded)

Marie Absolutely not, Ruth. We absolutely carry on. This is only a minor setback.

Ruth follows in her kit − a Westlife tour sweater and jogging bottoms

Ruth Really? I mean is it actually worth playing/ without ——
Marie Tuesday night is badminton night and will REMAIN badminton night regardless of whether or not Chris has disappeared to the Yorkshire Show with the badminton net.
Ruth Well I just presume they needed a net/ to ——
Marie It doesn't matter what they needed it for, Ruth. Like I said. We won't let it stop us.

Marie does some stretches, as Ruth gets her comparatively battered racquet out

PLAY.

Marie serves (practically over-arm) over no net. Not much chance to return it − didn't look totally legal to be honest. Whatever, Ruth misses

One love.
Ruth Sorry, would that have gone over/ the —— ?
Marie That would've gone over the net, yes. One love.
Ruth Well played.

Marie No, I must say I was sorry to miss the Yorkshire Show. I do enjoy it. It's one of the things I missed most when we were living in Cheshire.

Ruth No. Well. Yes.

Marie I mean they do HAVE a show, Cheshire. But it's —— (*scrunching her nose*) There's a fundamental difference, you see, Ruth. Yorkshire people go to the Yorkshire Show to see animals. Cheshire people go to the Cheshire Show to see other people from Cheshire. To preen. And peacock. And you know me, Ruth. The one thing I can't stand is snobbery.

Marie serves again, brutally, and wins the point

Two love.

Ruth (*picking up the shuttlecock*) Talking of Cheshire actually, Marie, I er ... (*waving loosely*) — wondering if you might have a word with Cora?

Marie She's not thinking of moving?

Ruth No, I mean she's having a tough time of it with her daughter at the moment. And even though it was a very different thing what happened to your Jenny, I ——

Marie (*in like lightning*) You didn't mention anything?

Ruth Oh no ——

Marie To Cora?

Ruth NO, of ——

Marie To anyone?

Ruth —course. I never have. I NEVER have. I ...

Ruth hands Marie back the shuttlecock

Two love.

Marie goes to her serving square, brooding, instead of serving

Marie What happened with Jenny is actually a perfect illustration of Cheshire as a whole. (*She preens the shuttlecock*) In Yorkshire ... In *Yorkshire* the story would've been "teacher seduces sixth form girl". In Cheshire, in a private school, it was "young slut leads astray brilliant head of physics who had a ninety per cent A-star pass rate." And the *moment*, Ruth, from THAT ... (*she clicks her fingers*) ... moment, the doors shut like —— (*Beat*) We might as well have been tinkers. We might as well have been going round Wilmslow selling lucky heather. (*Calm, calm*) Yorkshire's just got a better class of person. (*Putting*

her arm up to serve) Few notable exceptions of course ... (*She goes to serve, but doesn't*) ... although I've decided not to make an issue of the calendar.
Ruth Oh right. Oh *good*. I think in fairness Chris just/ wanted ——
Marie For you, to be honest, Ruth. (*She readies to serve*) I know you didn't want to do it. But Chris —— (*She bites it back*) You're a very accommodating person. Sometimes it's the ones who are accommodating who get taken advantage of.

Pause. This seems to strike Ruth hard

Marie serves. Ruth, in an unnatural spasm of grit, plays a great return

Ruth (*grittedly victorious*) Yes.
Marie Actually, Ruth, I think that would have gone in the net. (*Or, if Ruth misses:*) *Ruth, d'you think it's time you had some lessons?*

Suddenly the door flies open and Chris backs in, wheeling one end of a badminton net, either post of which have been made into sunflowers, and on whose net have been pegged bright pieces of card spelling the words "WI CALENDAR". Annie follows, pushing the other post

Chris (*on high octane*) ... OH MY GOD! *ELEVEN* CALENDARS?
Annie He bought one for each of his cricket team!
Chris NO!
Annie *Seriously!*
Chris That is UNBELIEVABLE! I mean —— (*Seeing Marie*) Marie!
Annie Oh God. "Tuesday badminton". Marie, we should have said we were borrowing the net.
Chris (*cursorily*) Oh right. Sorry, Marie. HEYY! Ruth! You know what happened today at the Yorkshire Show?
Ruth (*really uncomfortable*) Yes. No.
Chris We sold out of calendars in thirty-eight *minutes*!
Annie This woman bought the last five and there was practically a fist fight in the queue!
Ruth That's incredible!
Chris Honestly, Ruth, it was/ just ——
Annie You should've been there!

Celia and Cora burst in, Cora carrying a wicker basket

Celia There is a gentleman out here who has driven from *North Wales* to get a calendar today, only to find we'd sold out.

Cora (*proffering the basket*) Well put his address with the other four hundred.

Celia Aw c'mon. We can't send him home empty-handed —

Cora Tell you what. Why don't you nip out the back with a couple of bakewell tarts and do him a quick polaroid.

Celia (*gesturing to the others*) You see this jealousy? 'Cause he only recognized me?

Cora Hey. If I'd been shoving a piano he'd've recognized *me*.

Marie (*zipping up her racquet*) Anyway.

Chris Tell you what, I think we could be looking at that settee in the leather.

Annie Yeah, except then we'll have to ask High Ghyll to do a calendar to raise funds for your flower shop.

Marie Oh I'm fairly sure you won't find anyone at High Ghyll willing to pose naked. Good-night, Ruth.

Marie zips up her bag and heads out

Chris Actually, Marie, it's not "naked". It's "nude".

Ruth (*super-cheerful, sensing trouble like a meercat*) Good-night, Marie-e!

Chris I'm sure you'd appreciate the distinction. (*Smiling, for the girls' benefit*) Having frequented many a Cheshire art gallery.

Marie is almost out of the door but this shot brings her back

Marie "Art"? (*She turns*) Sorry I'm — (*wincing, archly*) — slightly lost. This is "you, naked behind a fruit loaf"?

The hall goes quiet. The others are suddenly an unwitting sports crowd

Ruth Actually, Chris is the "flower arranging"/ pose —

Marie I can't recall — I'm thinkin-ng and n-no, the Lady Lever Gallery does not have any watercolours of middle-aged women obscuring their pudenda with danish pastries.

Annie (*making light*) It's got some of women who look like they've eaten a few ...

Some of the girls laugh to try and make light too

Marie Perhaps the Pre-Raphaelites had figured out it might look slightly —

Ruth (*"aren't we having a lovely time"*) ANYWAY-Y...

Chris (*frowning slightly*) Sorry, Marie, do go on.

Marie — embarrassing.

Oo. Game on. The impromptu crowd turns to see how it will be volleyed

Chris Is that — "embarrassing" to us, or to you?
Marie Both.
Annie I'll lock up/ anyw —
Chris Marie, maybe our calendar sums up the spirit of the WI better than a load of wet bridges.

Oo

Marie More than the natural beauty of this county?
Chris Yes. That's Yorkshire by the way. The county you loved so much you went to live in Cheshire.

Beat

Marie And well done for staying here, Chris. Well done for staying put in the flower shop. Which is of course what all this is all about, isn't it? Really? The golden girl who was Dorothy in *The Wizard Of Oz*. The girl who everyone thought would be a weather girl. The girl who performed in the pencil skirt at the French Evening and got all the lads' tongues lolling and ended up in a flower shop on the Skipton Road and is now just *desperate* for a bit of the front of the stage again? Not a whole play, by the way. Not the hard work, line-learning — God, that takes following things through. No, it's just the little front-of-curtains — (*putting her arms out*) "Pow"! The little shot of "look at me, I'm doing t'ai chi!" "Pow! I'm organizing a vodka night."

Every word is true and Chris knows it

Chris (*swallowing hard*) I am doing this —
Marie TELL me that's not what makes your heart beat faster about this calendar, Chris Harper/ tell —
Chris — for John Clarke I am doing this —
Marie Tell me.
Chris — and because of him and because he would have laughed his bloody socks off —
Marie Tell me.
Chris — and because I can hear that laughter now —
Marie TELL ME!
Ruth (*shouting*) CELIA.

To stop the fight, Ruth pulls a calendar from her bag. It has a red ribbon on it, tied up ready to give to someone

Cora Christ almighty, Ruth. I thought that was a Kalashnikov.
Ruth It's a calendar. For the man. The Wales man. Outside.

Pause

Marie (*quietly*) Good-night, Ruth.
Annie (*oil on the waters*) Night, Marie.

Marie withdraws and leaves

Celia Isn't that yours for My Eddie?
Ruth It's fine. It *was*, but it's fine.
Celia My Eddie doesn't want it?

Chris takes it, so she too can leave

Chris I'll take it.

Chris exits

The exchange of fire has left Celia, Annie, Cora and Ruth rather stunned

Cora Not been playing golf recently have you, Ceel? I could do with
a vodka.
Celia As it happens I was out yesterday so I'm fully tooled up.
Annie Right. Well that was all a bit ——
Celia Hey hey hey. Times like this we have to get straight back on the
Harley!
Annie It's not what John would've wanted. (*She starts tidying the net*)
For everyone to start arguing ——
Celia Come on-n ...
Annie Maybe Marie's right. Maybe we *have* upset people/ who ——
Celia Good. Some people need upsetting.
Annie No, I mean ——
Celia I spend half my life with people who need upsetting.
Cora Shouldn't've joined a golf club.
Celia Cora, d'you think I planned to? I was *lured*. I was *lured* to Yorkshire
with all this "Ohh come back 'ome, love, let me take you back to
live in God's county." I agree, we move ... (*pointing*) ... Suddenly
he comes down with this disease called "Golf". And it's terminal.
Suddenly if I want to see him it means spending half my life with a
group of women who — sorry, "*ladies*" — who pathologically make
rules to make sure *no one* gets upset! Rules for the putting green. And
the locker room! And the car park. And the bar. And — God's SAKE

— "Conversation Codes for the Captain's dinner" so we don't stray off the subject of golf when all you can basically say about golf is, "I didn't hit it straight so it missed the hole but if I had've hit it straight it would've gone in the hole."

Cora I think you might need some counselling about this, Ceel.

Celia And of course all the stuff they really want to say still gets said. Just behind people's backs. Usually mine.

Beat

Ruth (*tentatively*) What kind of/ thing —— ?

Celia That I dress like a tart.

Ruth *No.*

Cora In fairness, you do a bit, Ceel.

Ruth CORA.

Cora No, I'm just saying — Celia's front is never backwards in coming forwards.

Celia And DAMN right it isn't. Which is exactly how it should be. Y'r breasts aren't something that should get hidden away for some bloody social — pathetic — whatever — reason but I tell you what, thanks to women like the bloody golf club girls they ARE. And if my mum hadn't been too mortified to show doctors her breasts when the time came, we'd still have the rest of her. (*Beat*) Which is why what I'd like to say to the Hermes mafia of the Ladies' Bar is, "Get down to the WI, girls. Come and hang out with the real women of this county and learn a little debauchery before it's too bloody late." Cheers.

Jessie walks in the kitchen doorway with a letter in her hand

Jessie Has everyone just walked past this that came through the letterbox?

Cora This place has a letterbox?

Jessie (*reading it*) "Alternative WI Calendar, Yorkshire."

Annie It never got here addressed like that?

Jessie (*reading*) "Your calendar was the first time I've smiled in fifteen months."

Immediately everyone stops

(*Reading*) "My husband never understood why I joined the WI. But I think if he ..." (*She pauses. She hands it to Annie*)

Annie (*reading*) "But I think if he had lived to see these photographs he would have understood in a second."

Music plays

A piece of paper falls from above in the hall like a flake of snow. As Annie continues reading, our focus is drawn to a new letter falling. Over the music, Ruth goes and picks it up off the floor, as a letter off a doormat.

Ruth (*reading*) "Dear Girls of the Alternative Calendar. I first saw your photos sitting in a relatives' room, probably on a settee very much like the one you are trying to buy."

It starts to rain letters into the hall, like a light fall of snow

Jessie (*reading one of the letters*) "... it took such bravery. Which of course is the one thing Danny had so much of. To be told at sixteen you would never be eighteen would have wiped the smile from anyone's face. But with him, it never quite did."

In pools of light, the girls pick up letters and read, overlapping, so that with the snow fall, there is an accompanying word fall

Cora (*reading*) " ... she would have laughed out loud at seeing your photographs, and would have put your calendar right up there on the wall beside —— "

Celia (*reading*) "I am currently in the high security wing of Her Majesty's Prison, Barlinnie, and was mightily impressed by the sheer size of your —— " (*She snaps it shut*)

The girls are picking up other letters around them

Annie (*reading*) "... the unexpected release of being able to see the word 'leukaemia' printed somewhere and not feel my fingertips go one degree colder ..."

Ruth (*reading*) "In January, my mummy —— " (*No, no, can't read any more*)

Jessie (*reading*) " ... my GOD she'd've been the first one behind the buns to beat the disease. Because the truth is she'd tried everything else —— "

The music takes over the word fall, as they pick up letters, only being broken by:

Celia (*reading*) "I have recently been released from Barlinnie Prison —— " Oh my GOD.

SCENE 5

The church hall. Later the same day

The door suddenly flies open, revealing Chris pulling a clothes rack on wheels. It bears several black suit protectors, clearly with dresses in

Chris AAARGH! Ladies! Give me a hand here?
Everyone (*variously*) WHOA my GOD! *CHRIS!* STEADY-Y! (*Etc.*)

The music stops. The girls all rush to help Chris

Chris Ladies, I have just set a world record for Knapeley. In ONE morning, I've done three radio interviews, PLUS a magazine ——
Cora Did they not want to talk to all of us?
Chris They — yes. They will eventually. PLUS, STANDBY. STANDBY FOR THE BIG ONE! ANNIE? (*She takes centre stage*) I have recently been exchanging phone calls with a very nice lady in *London*, OK, who has asked if we'd agree ... Annie, are you getting this? ... Tomorrow, OK, in this church hall ... to be on *television!*

There is considerable surprise and excitement in the hall

Celia NO! (*She puts her hand to her mouth*) No no no no ...!
Cora What, you mean like in an interview?
Jessie Who with?
Chris No no, a commercial!
Annie For the calendar?
Chris Now just imagine how THAT's going to raise the profile! Honest to God, we'll have to reprint!

There is MUCH joy in the room!

Cora		That is just ——
Celia	(*together*)	Wow!
Ruth		Oh Chris that is just ——
Jessie		I don't BELIEVE this ——

Chris They're sending a *beautician* out — look — from the Craven Health Spa ...

Chris gives a pink business card to Celia, who hands it to Ruth. Ruth looks at it intently

And this is the best bit — how about THIS? I suddenly think "there's a move to be made here." Straight on the phone to Dickens and Bent in Skipton. "Hello, Miss October here." (*Pointing*) Knew *exactly* who I was! "Going to be appearing on television, how's about you making a little donation to the cause ...?" (*She unzips one of the suiters*) Ta-daa! (*She unleashes a chic black dress*)

Jessie Oh now *hell-o.*

Celia They're not Pellegrini ...? (*She checks the label*) Oh my God! They're Gina Pellegrini!

Chris What did I tell you? Coordinated image! Picked up like THAT! Go on. Try them on. We've got to phone back any changes.

Celia, Cora and Jessie exit into the kitchen with some excitement and cross-chat

Ruth is still looking at the card intently, so Chris puts a triumphant arm round her

Chris (*to Annie, indicating Ruth*) Look at this! Stunned to silence! Top drawer, that, isn't it Ruth, hey? The Craven Health Spa? Isn't that where Eddie goes?

Beat

Ruth (*finding a smile*) Yeah. Yeah, it's er ——

Chris (*herding Ruth off*) Go on, go on, get those measurements! Annie!

Ruth exits

(*Honing in on Annie*) Annie-e! What d'you think?

Annie (*quietly*) It's happened to them.

Chris What?

Annie shows her a letter

Annie Just like it happened to me.

Chris takes a letter and looks at it

What do I say? I mean, I can't not ... (*"Respond". Beat*) It's like they've written to me for help.

Chris You *are* helping them. You did a calendar, remember?

Rod (*off*) LADIES AND GENTLEMEN ...

Rod enters with a bunch of sunflowers

Rod It's Mister October!
Chris Rod ——

Rod grabs Chris and hugs her

Rod Has anyone ever told you, you're the most b-yyyoootiful wife a man could/ ever —— ?
Chris (*being hugged*) Rod what are you playing at?
Rod So what, a husband's not allowed to buy his wife a bouquet now, for a celebration? Where d'you want them? (*He heads towards the kitchen*)
Chris Rod, you can't —— (*She pulls him back*) There's naked women out there.
Rod Love, it's Knapeley. There's naked women everywhere. (*He winks*) Hey, Annie.
Annie (*slightly embarrassed*) Hi, Rod.
Chris We had these in the shop?
Rod (*dropping his head in mock shame*) I had to go to Tesco. (*To Annie*) John wouldn't bloody approve of THAT, would he, eh? David has bought these from the hand of Goliath.
Annie They're beautiful.
Chris How did you know?
Rod What?
Chris (*confused*) You said you bought these to celebrate ——
Rod I did! To celebrate the fact that somewhere out there across the dales of Yorkshire, a manufacturer of personalized wedding cakes has come down with a summer cold!
Chris (*slightly irritated*) What?
Rod (*holding up a necktag*) ... and has consequently pulled out of the Northern Bridal Fair in Leeds! We're in! (*Putting it on himself*) Tomorrow my darling we are stand number two-one-nine!
Chris No, "we" can't be. "We're" going on *television*!
Rod What?
Chris Isn't it great?

Beat

Rod Right. But at these fairs you're better at all the actual selling, "meeting people" stuff. You're just ... (*Feeling awkward in front of Annie. He smiles at her*) She's fantastic at that.
Chris Rod! (*As if this explains everything*) It's TELEVISION!

Rod (*suddenly hard as nails*) Chris, we're going to the bridal fair. We don't have the luxury *not* to.

Chris knows they don't. But she wants that TV so badly

Chris looks at Rod and his flowers but has no words. So she just leaves. And leaves behind a rather messy silence

Annie looks at Rod, who is clearly slightly wounded by this

Annie We'll be fine, Rod. She doesn't have to be here.
Rod But I want her to be here, Annie. That's the thing. I want her to have all this. (*He just about finds a smile for Annie*) Never make a business out of something you love. I go for a walk now up Grizedale, see all the flowers and I think, "It's you little bastards who are screwing us over." (*He looks to the sunflowers*) Then again, John managed it, didn't he? (*Beat*) Worked that park for thirty years, never *stopped* banging on about how beautiful it was. Couldn't bloody shut him up.

Annie lets this settle. It's true

Annie Rod, how bad ARE things with the shop?

Pause

Rod Try and keep 'em cool.

Rod leaves. That's answer enough

Annie watches where he went for a beat, then takes the sunflowers out

SCENE 6

The church hall. The next day

New day. New girl. Elaine enters, a younger beautician, stunningly white in a pharmaceutical dress

Elaine No no no no, this is fine, ladies, there's enough light in here. We'll do it in here.

Ruth and Jessie enter from the kitchen. They have paper collar-protectors round their necks

(*Steering Jessie to a chair*) This is where they're going to be filming you so if you look all right in here, we're winning aren't we, hey?! Just wait one second. I'll get the magic make-up.

Elaine exits

Ruth and Jessie watch her go

Jessie D'you think people like her get a kick out of treating people like they're Special Needs? D'you reckon it's some kind of psychological inversion that makes her feel younger if she treats everyone else like they're senile?

Ruth Well I suppose in fairness she/ just ——

Jessie Ruth, I have never met anyone who uses the phrase "in fairness" as much as you do.

Ruth Well, I'm sorry,/ I ——

Jessie No no, don't apologize. It's not wrong. It's the better way. (*She fiddles with her collar*) Don't get drawn into agreeing with my bitter ruminations. That's just me, grown venomous by years of exposure to schoolchildren. (*She rubs Ruth's arm and smiles*) Much softer is our Ruth.

Elaine returns with her magic box

Elaine Right. HERE we are, ladies-s! How are we *doing*?

Jessie (*in a gummy senile way*) Who's moved me television?

Elaine (*stopping and frowning*) What was that?

Jessie Never mind. (*She nods at Ruth*) Do her first. I'm going round the back to score some crack.

Jessie leaves

Elaine (*a little confused*) Right-t. SO. Let's just pop yourself down on that-t, my love, make you comfy. (*On autopilot she produces a pink business card*) I'm Elaine from the Craven Health Spa-a ... (*She offers Ruth the card*) There's my card.

Ruth I've already got one.

Elaine Lovely. What I'm going to be doing for the television is a little basic T-Zone and A-Zone. Have you ever had that done before?

Ruth No.

Elaine Oh, you'll love it. 'Cause you're the lady — wasn't it the organizer, Chris, wasn't she telling me they were all going to do it and you WEREN'T and then you suddenly changed your mind at the last minute? Is that right?

Ruth doesn't reply

Suddenly got the confidence up! It's funny how that happens, isn't it? You know, a lot of ladies find that when they've had our "Dead Sea Salt treatment", they get this (*gesturing loosely*) inner kind of — "wha"? To do things!

Ruth Possibly.

Elaine Absolutely.

Ruth Although I think with me it was likely more finding your underwear in the map pocket of Eddie's Peugeot.

Pause. Elaine stops the beauty treatment

You know? The little red ones? I mean I'm not surprised you didn't notice you hadn't got them on afterwards, they couldn't't've provided much insulation. But there was one of these? Little business card. Must've fallen out of your bag in the whole ... (*she "smiles"*) ... mêlée, you know? And that's when I thought, "Well maybe he'd see me in a different light if I went and did this calendar!" Pointlessly, as it turns out. 'Cause what I hadn't realized is that a woman who takes her clothes off on a calendar is a "tart" whereas one who does it in a lay-by is a really good sport. But hey. (*She stands*) What I DID get to realize is that Eddie Reynoldson is one of those guys who wouldn't understand beauty if it was staring him in the face. And you know how I worked that out, love? (*Beat*) Because it was. Now in fairness fuck off back to him.

Elaine exits in record time

(*To herself, in total disbelief*) I did it!

Celia bursts in, wearing her new black dress, ahead of Cora, in a swirl of excitement and cross-talk

Celia No, but they say that, don't they?

Cora That's rubbish.

Celia Honestly, they say that about television. The camera puts about ten pounds on you.

Cora Let's hope there's only one bloody camera.

Jessie bobs round the door with some urgency

Jessie Girls!

Cora }
Celia } (*together; standing to attention*) Yes, Miss Raistrick!

Jessie (*delivering urgent headlines to the girls about what to expect:*) Annie. DON'T say anything. Looks a little unkempt. (*Calmly calling back to Annie*) Everyone's in here, my dear. In you come!

Jessie ushers Annie in — looking a total wreck; dress crumpled, hair awry

Cora God al-*mighty* —

Jessie coughs sharply

You look great! Doesn't she look great?
Jessie I found her asleep on a pew.
Ruth You what?
Celia In *church*?
Annie Look, don't —— (*"get worried"*) It was just — I went to put some sunflowers in, to keep them cool. And then I thought I'd start replying to some of the letters, you know? That we were sent?
Jessie Whatever. I think you'd better have first go with the make-up girl.
Ruth I think tragically she might've just left.
Celia } (*together*) { You're JOKING!
Cora } { WHAT?
Annie Oh my GOD ...

Liam the shoot director enters, a young man wearied by his current mission and the general lack of achievement of any of his dreams

Liam Ladies, good-afternoon. My name's Liam, I'm from KPL. You're my six stars for the commercial, yeah?
Annie Liam I'm sorry — my make-up! I haven't had a chance/ to ——
Liam No worries. Calm, calm ... Wardrobe's back here.

He checks the ceiling lights which clearly aren't to his satisfaction

Annie And it's only five of us. Chris can't make it.

This is the first the others have heard of that

Celia } (*together*) { What?
Ruth } { Seriously?
Cora Chris isn't COMING?
Liam No worries. Five's enough. I'm just —— (*Looking round the ceiling*) It's not GREAT for lighting, this place, is it?

Liam escorts Annie out

The others look a bit leaderless

Cora We'll manage! I'll give us a bit of a build-up. Bit of — (*à la Blueberry Hill*)
And did those feet — do do dooby do ...
Ruth Don't mess round with religious songs!
Jessie (*"excuse me"*) Ap-ap. Remember what John said. (*Gesturing at "being part of the same thing"*) "Religion, blues, they're all ..."
Cora Eh it's sodding dangerous though, if you end up a church organist, Jess. Seriously, no word of a lie, one time, someone's funeral, Dad's in the pulpit, I'm playing on grief autopilot — (*She starts plonking out "Dear Lord And Father Of Mankind" on the piano like a steamhammer. Singing*) "Dear Lord and Father Of Mankind ——" (*Speaking*) Suddenly I look down at Ruby in her carry-cot and honest to God, next thing I know I'm playing —— (*She starts playing "Stormy Weather" and sings the first two lines; then, speaking*) Turned round, the whole congregation are looking at me like "What the HELL —— ?" (*She continues singing the next line of "Stormy Weather"*)

This causes a slight pause

Celia Why *did* you lose touch?

Cora sings the next line of "Stormy Weather"

Ruby's dad. It always sounds like you loved him.

Beat. She did

Cora I lost touch in return for board and lodging. Which is what happens. If you're young and pregnant. And scared. (*Beat*) And your father's a vicar who professes to love all men but when it comes down to it not actually black Americans that much.
Ruth Have you not just *told* Ruby this?
Cora (*"yes"*) Oh God, Ruth. But end of the day she wants to find her dad. An' I don't blame her. An' believe me it's not for want of trying.

Liam enters, talking into a walkie talkie

Liam OK, ANDY! LET THERE BE LIGHT!

Very bright lights come on. There are clearly some technical guys out back making this happen

Now we're getting somewhere. Oh and look who I found!

Chris enters and strikes a pose in the doorway, looking like something out of the Folies Bergère

Liam exits

Chris Well, girls. Do we look something else or WHAT?!
Cora Ha HEY!
Celia }
Ruth } *(together)* CHRIS-S!
Jessie Oh now here she IS!
Ruth *(calling)* ANNIE? CHRIS MADE IT!
Chris Isn't this — just — fantastic!
Ruth Chris, Annie's just —
Chris OK now. Important. *(She claps, slightly Marie-like)* Can you remember the pose? That kind of "leaning-back" thing, left foot forward, right arm back and smile —

Annie enters in her dress. She stops dead

Annie Chris?
Chris Oh, Annie, can you come over here?
Annie *(doing no such thing)* Why aren't you at the bridal fair?
Chris I'm not there because —
Annie Where's Rod?
Chris *(slightly irritated)* He's — just ... *(to the girls)* Girls, have a little practice.

Chris scoops Annie off to privacy

I'm not there because of John, Annie. To be honest. Because I woke up this morning and asked myself, what's more important? That we raise enough for that settee or that some drippy girl from Hull gets a lily-of-the-valley bridal posy? Wasn't much of a competition. John comes first.
Annie Does he?
Chris *(stopping, turning)* What's that supposed to mean?

Liam returns with a handful of dayglo sunflowers. They are garish and unpleasantly false — bright, shiny plastic, almost comic in intent,

arranged in groups of three, two higher, one lower. They are in fact
a girdle which fit over a naked female form, covering modesty in an
effective but rather picture-postcard way

Liam Right let's get this started. Here we go with your sunflowers!
Ruth (*tapping one*) Oh now — isn't that clever? Is it plastic or are
they —— ?
Cora (*hanging one on some furniture*) What are they for, are they
decoration? Kinda hanging about the place? Some sort of "theme"?
Liam They certainly are. Do they fit?

Liam hangs one on Annie

Everyone (*variously*) Oh my God/ look at that!
Cora They hang on us!
Liam Yeah. One for each of you, except Chris who's actually gonna be
holding the product.
Annie The calendar?
Liam The washing powder.

Pause

Jessie The "washing powder"?
Celia What "washing powder"?
Ruth Is this advert not about the calendar?
Chris 'Course it is. Long term. Just imagine what it's going to do for
the profile —— !
Liam OK I promise this won't take long. (*He smiles*) Once we've cranked
up the lights, it'll be off with your kit, couple of clicks, done.
Jessie (*at Chris* — *"what?"*) Sorry?
Liam Andy?

Liam is about to go off, as the girls all look in horror at each other

Chris Sorry, Liam. You want us — with these, over —— ?
Liam The caption's gonna go over, yeah. "We'd rather go naked than
use another ..." You know? You get the picture!

There is a pause

Chris These flowers, but *without* the dresses?

Liam looks around them, finally understanding the hesitancy

Liam I mean that's not a problem, is it? Stripping off? I mean, that is what you "do"?

A beat. Chris has to turn to her troops and put on a brave face. None of them WERE aware this was the score

Chris Absolutely!
Liam Absolutely! (*Into his walkie talkie*) Andy? Take these lights up forty percent.

Liam goes

There is a pause

Chris Right. OK. I hadn't realized.

Beat. A ferocious key light comes on. Unsympathetic, hard, it is the antithesis of the light the night they took the photos in here. They all wince

OK.
Ruth Right. Well ——

Chris leads from the front and starts to undo her clothing

Annie Don't touch a button.
Chris Annie/ just ——
Annie Put your coats on. We're out of here.

The girls don't know what to do

Do NOT touch ONE *BUTTON*.
Chris (*out of the side of her mouth, gesturing "carry on"*) Girls ...

Cora, Ruth, Jessie and Celia de-flower themselves and leave, murmuring "sorry", slightly on eggshells

Is there a problem?

Annie doesn't answer. She packs

Yes?

Annie doesn't answer

Are you going to answer m — ?
Annie Please don't ask me if there's a problem, Chris, when we're selling soap wearing dayglo sunflowers.
Chris For a photoshoot, I am. For John.

Annie snorts a little laugh

(*Getting narked*) What?
Annie "For John." That's good. That you still think that.
Chris Yes. I do. And I think John'd think you were acting —
Annie Let me tell you what *I* think John'd think, OK? "Annie, you're a woman who once took her clothes off because of me, and who now takes them off because 'that's what she does'."
Chris Is this 'cause I've organized it? Got us a sponsor. Finally followed through on something? Finally made this calendar a success?
Annie No, y'see what's actually happened, Chris, what's *actually* happened is that this calendar's made YOU a success.

This hurts

Chris And not YOU of course? Not bloody — Florence Nightingale. Sleeping in churches. Answering letters. LOADS of people lose partners to this disease. I bet THEY don't get FAN MAIL. Wouldn't you say THAT's made YOU a "success"? A very successful ... "bereaved woman"? A — a — a "celebrity widow"? (*Beat*) "Saint Annie of Knapeley?" Eh? (*Beat*) Hey?
Annie I'm not a saint. Because I would rob every penny of this calendar to buy one more hour with him. (*Beat*) And you've still got yours.

Annie starts to cry. And it's the crying she always needed to do

(*In tears*) And you're here!

Chris was the cloudbuster, who now can't go to her because of the Grand Canyon that's opened up between them

Annie leaves

Liam comes in

Liam Hello?

Chris (*attempting a brave face*) I think — might be a problem with some of the er ... (*She dries up*)

Liam assesses the situation

Liam Right. Well. (*Beat*) Looks like it's just you. (*He clears the other "sunflower" girdles*) I'll let the agency know but they'll be cool with that. End of the day all they want is someone from the WI, nude. That's all it's about, isn't it, all this? That's the — *frisson*. ANDY, CAN YOU CLEAR THE KITCHEN? (*To Chris*) Little bit of privacy. (*He hands her the washing powder*) You cool with it? Being just "you"? (*Smiling*) Don't mind being the "star"?

Liam goes

Chris (*quietly*) I never have.

Chris goes off

Music plays: "Jerusalem"

SCENE 7

The church hall. Late summer

Cora, Jessie, Celia, Annie and Marie enter, singing a multi-part vocal arrangement of "Jerusalem" over the music

The girls are dressed in summery clothes and singing with optimism and verve. Under Cora's instruction, the song is transformed — as though they've remembered how beautiful it was. Marie leads them on. Celia, Jessie, Annie and Cora seem to be dressed light and liberated somehow. Maybe it's just a new self-confidence they exert

Everyone (*singing*) And did those feet in ancient time
　　　　　Walk upon England's mountains green?
　　　　　And was the holy lamb of God
　　　　　On England's pleasant pastures seen?

　　　　　And did the countenance divine
　　　　　Shine forth upon our clouded hills?
　　　　　And was Jerusalem builded here
　　　　　Among those dark satanic mills?

That was fab

Marie That's coming along.

The girls sit

Ruth rushes in. She looks totally transformed: new hair, less damage-limitation clothing

Ruth He went past! He drove right past me! Honestly, Marie, I was stood waving, I couldn't've been waving more clearly.
Marie Oh for GOODNESS' sake. I gave QUITE clear directions ... (*Pause*) Ladies, it looks like we may NOT have a talk from Brian Hickox on "Land Reclamation On The Isle Of Mull".
Everyone (*sighing pointedly*) Awww.
Marie I'll just go and check.

Marie goes out

Ruth (*when Marie has gone*) I didn't wave! I saw him go and I didn't wave!

Cora, Celia, Jessie and Annie all pat her back and hug her with various "well done"s

Celia ⎫   ⎧ Well done Ruth!
Cora ⎬ (*together*) ⎨ Nice one.
Jessie ⎭   ⎩ That's my girl.
Ruth I feel terrible. That's the kind of thing Chris'd do.

Intended warmly, this seems to create a slight chill in the room

Jessie Is Chris ...? Is she missing it again tonight?

There's a beat

Annie Haven't spoken.

Marie enters

Marie Stupid man. (*Louder*) Right. We'll have to just get on with the notices. (*She opens a diary*) Number one. "Cora".
Cora (*standing, taking her time*) In this week's consignment of letters I got one from America.

Jessie We've had lots of letters from America, love.

Cora But this one is from a man who has a very dull job in a college, teaching music. But who'd recognized me from a photograph in the *Boston Herald*. And was "pleased to see after all these years that his old flame from Leeds University had kept on rocking."

Celia Oh my God. Is that Ruby's dad?

Cora (*unable to hide her smile*) In response to this I'd like to announce that on Thursday there'll be the first ever rehearsal of the new Knapeley Rhythm and Blues Choir. In here. Eight o' clock. Bring a bottle.

Marie (*taking a beat*) Right. Notice number two. (*Reading the entry*) "Ruth"?

Ruth (*standing*) Right. Yes I'd like to say that I just *wanted* to say I'd like to offer a talk for January, if you'd like, to do a talk. (*Nodding affirmation to herself*) Yes.

Marie (*slight pause*) D'you have a title?

Ruth "Up The Zambezi In A Canoe."

They all look at her

Celia Have you been up the Zambezi in a canoe?

Ruth No. But if I don't commit to the speech, I'll not do it.

She sits. Marie looks down at the diary

Marie R-right. Notice number three. (*She peers at the diary*) Is this a mistake ...?

Ruth (*standing again*) No, it *is* me again. I was just wondering if anyone fancied coming up the Zambezi in a canoe. It's an organized trip in the Sunday Supplement so ——

Marie Ruth ——

Jessie Doesn't the Zambezi have those little fishes that swim up your doo-dah?

Ruth (*horrified*) Has it?

Marie Ladies.

Ruth Maybe I'll just go up the Avon.

Marie LADIES, PLEASE.

It seems ALL the girls are now behaving as Chris and Annie once did

(*Reading*) Finally, "Annie".

They all look to Annie

Annie *I* haven't.

Marie "To read out". From Chris.

Marie hands a letter to Annie. She cautiously takes and opens it

Annie (*reading*) "The first sales figures for the Knapeley Alternative WI
Calendar have just been forwarded from Leukaemia Research. The
target, to buy a settee for the relatives' room at Skipton General, was
five hundred and nineteen pounds. As of August ninth, the calendar
has raised five hundred and eighty ... thousand pounds."

Celia ⎫   ⎧ (*hand to mouth*) No! No no NO-O!
Jessie ⎬ (*together*) ⎨ *Thousand*?
Ruth ⎭   ⎩ (*nearly swearing*) Oh my ——

Cora (*loudly, over this*) What else does she say?

Annie (*reading*) "Unable to locate a settee costing this much, even in
Harrogate, Skipton General have accepted the surplus money as a gift.

*In this moment, Chris appears at the church hall door, unseen, as if
unsure of her welcome in this place*

As a result, next year the John Clarke Memorial Settee will ... will ..."
(*She can't go on*)

Chris Will sit in the newly-named "John Clarke Memorial Wing."

Chris approaches. On glass. And hangdog

Marie, I thought you might like to know Rod and I just delivered some
bulrushes to High Ghyll WI.

Marie (*coldly*) Really.

Chris Apparently next year they're planning on doing a nude calendar.

There is a pause

Marie (*exploding and fisting the air*) OH YES. ONE-NIL. *BLOODY
BRILLIANT* ... (*She recomposes and the other Marie reclaims
control*) Well, that's interesting. So. In the absence of our speaker I'm
afraid, girls, we're left with absolutely nothing/ for this evening ——

Chris I could do some t'ai chi.

The girls react with some cynicism, simultaneously

Celia ⎫   ⎧ Oh aye ...
Jessie ⎪   ⎪ Yeah yeah yeah ...
Ruth ⎬ (*together*) ⎨ Chris-s ...
Cora ⎭   ⎩ You know, she doesn't give up.

Chris No I finished that book on t'ai chi. Actually read it, you know. Properly.

The girls look at Marie

Marie You know what, Chris? Frankly I'm past caring. Annie — congratulations. If anyone wants me I'll be in the *Ram's Head* at High Ghyll with two buns and a bottle of Bollinger.

Marie goes out

The vibe in the hall is uncertain. The girls look at each other ... and rise to clear the chairs

All except Annie. Chris looks to her. Annie is well aware that this is an olive branch in itself

Annie You realize if you'd done that commercial you'd've been the most famous WI woman in history.
Chris The scent wasn't flowers of Yorkshire. John would've killed me. (*Beat*) And it's his calendar. Not mine.

This last line goes a long way as an apology for Annie

I was thinking we could maybe go up on John's hill.

Beat

Annie Don't you think we've embarrassed ourselves enough up there?

Beat. Chris looks at her

Chris I think you should see it.

Beat

Annie (*nodding*) All right.
Chris Ladies?

Chris starts doing the "Heaven and Earth". The girls join in

(*To Annie*) I didn't mean to call you a saint.
Annie (*after a beat*) I know. I absolve you, my child.

Music plays. Over this, and over a sequence of fluid, beautiful t'ai chi moves the scene change takes place

SCENE 8

John's hill. Half an hour later

We are one final time on John's hill. And it's a field of sunflowers. And it's magical. The girls stand amongst the sunflowers

Cora Turned out all right didn't they?
Ruth John's seeds.
Jessie They turned out fine.
Celia Should be proud, Annie.

Beat

Annie I think we all should be.

Chris looks privately to Annie

Cora T'ai chi in the middle of his sunflowers. What d'you think John would've said about that?

They all instinctively look to Chris for a response. She gives the moment to Annie

Annie (*as John*) "Sod it, girls. Go and get some chips."

Music plays. The girls walk over the hill

   Cora, Celia, Ruth and Jessie exit

Chris and Annie stop at the prow of the hill, and turn to look at the sunflowers. Annie offers the hug. Chris takes it

We are left with them in a field of sunflowers, swaying gently in the Yorkshire breeze, looking for sunlight. Just flowers

Flowers, flowers, flowers

Black-out

FURNITURE AND PROPERTY LIST

ACT I
SCENE 1

On stage: Piano. *On it*: CD player
Piano stool
Coat stand with coats hung on it
Shot glasses
Covered box. *In it*: five fir cones decorated to look like a boyband (sitting on miniature "stools" in white "jackets" with "microphones")
Mirror on wall
Hatch that opens outwards from kitchen area
Megaphone
Slide projector (practical)
Six chairs
Badminton court marked out on floor

Off stage: Paper bag containing sunflower seeds (in pocket) (**Chris**)
Large glass flagon full of "home brew", gas candle-lighter pen (in pocket) (**John**)

SCENE 2

Off stage: Candle lamp on a stick (**Marie**)
1970s torch taped to an old golf club (**Cora**)
Makeshift lantern (**Jessie**)
Fake handbell (**Ruth**)
Victorian lantern (**Annie**)

SCENE 3

Off stage: Flowers and a half-hearted "basket" (**Jessie**)
Bottled beers on tray decorated as Montego Bay with cotton reels and Ferrero Rocher wrappers (**Chris**)
Cake tin (**Rod**)
Basket containing carton of fruit juice and rug (**Annie**)
Wheelchair, bottles of beer (**Celia/John**)
Trophy, blue sash (**Lady Cravenshire**)

Personal: **John**: white paper bag with writing on it (in pocket)

SCENE 4

Strike: **Jessie**'s flowers
Wheelchair

Set: Scenery/ backdrop for John's hill
Plastic bag. *In it*: small gold plaque; ripped-out page of a cata-
logue; selection of calendars
Fold-out microstool
Camera

SCENE 5

Strike: Scenery/backdrop for John's hill

Off stage: Scrabby art folder containing pages of sketches, including one
double page spread (**Lawrence**)

SCENE 6

Set: Huge teapot and china cup behind serving hatch doors

Off stage: Two studio lights, camera with practical remote flash attachment
on tripod, two reflector shields, catering trolley with tower of
cherry buns covered by sheet, box containing two balls of wool on
knitting needles, knitted sheet, shiny backdrop, six Santa Claus
hats, variety of Christmas wines, gift and cracker props, carol
sheets (**Lawrence** and **Rod**)
Golf trolley containing bottle of vodka; shot glasses (**Celia**)
Table with tablecloth that reaches down to the ground; oranges;
equipment for making marmalade. (**Lawrence** and **Cora**)
Two florists' buckets full of orchids (**Chris**)

Personal: **Chris**: bunch of straws, including one short

ACT II
SCENE 1

Strike: Props for photo shoot, golf trolley

Set: Small lectern with crude traffic-light warning system
Line micropone

SCENE 2

Strike: Lectern, line microphone

Set: Calendars

Personal: **Chris**: watch

SCENE 3

Set: Props from the photoshoot:

Off stage: Large funeral wreath of white carnations spelling "MUM"
                  (**Cora** and **Jessie**)
               Bag containing props from the photoshoot including teacup
                  and corsage (**Celia** and **Annie**)

SCENE 4

Off stage: Zip-up badminton bag containing flash badminton racquet in
                  zip-up case; shuttlecocks (**Marie**)
               Sports bag containing battered badminton racquet; calendar tied
                  up with a red ribbon (**Ruth**)
               Badminton net, either post of which have been made
                  into sunflowers, with bright pieces of card pegged on to
                  it spelling the words "WI CALENDAR" (**Chris** and **Annie**)
               Wicker basket (**Cora**)
               Letter (**Jessie**)
               Many more letters, which fall from the flies to create a "snowfall"
                  effect (**SM**)

SCENE 5

Off stage: Clothes rack on wheels containing chic black dresses in black suit
                  protectors; pink business card (**Chris**)
               Letter (**Annie**)
               Bunch of sunflowers; necktag for a trade fair (**Rod**)

SCENE 6

Off stage: Make-up box; pink business card (**Elaine**)
               Handful of bright, shiny plastic sunflowers, arranged in groups of
                  three, two higher, one lower, which fit over the female form as
                  girdles, walkie-talkie, box of washing powder (**Liam**)

Personal: **Ruth**: paper collar-protector
               Jessie: paper collar-protector

SCENE 7

Off stage: Diary, letter (**Marie**)

SCENE 8

Set: Scenery/ backdrop for John's hill
               Field of swaying sunflowers

LIGHTING PLOT

Practical fittings required: slide projector, two studio lights, camera with flash, traffic light warning system on lectern, overhead striplights

ACT I, Scene 1

To open: Darkness

Cue 1	**Cora**: (*singing*): "On England's pleasant pastures seen?" *Bring up general interior lighting*	(Page 1)
Cue 2	**Ruth** turns off the lights *Darken lighting*	(Page 5)
Cue 3	**Brenda Hulse** turns the projector on *A light shines from the projector on to the audience*	(Page 5)
Cue 4	**Brenda Hulse**: "... fascinating world ... of broccoli." *The light from the projector goes off and on again*	(Page 5)
Cue 5	**Brenda Hulse**: "... merely with the carrot." *The light from the projector changes to orange*	(Page 5)
Cue 6	**Brenda Hulse**: "Or sprout." *The light from the projector changes to green*	(Page 5)
Cue 7	**Brenda Hulse**: "...with *this* man." *The light from the projector changes back to white*	(Page 6)
Cue 8	**Brenda Hulse**: "The James Bond f —— " *Cut out light from the projector*	(Page 6)
Cue 9	**Ruth** leaps up and turns on the lights *Bring up general interior lighting*	(Page 6)

ACT I, Scene 2

To open: General interior lighting

No cues

ACT I, Scene 3

To open: General interior lighting

No cues

ACT I, Scene 4

To open: Exterior lighting, early summer

No cues

ACT I, Scene 5

To open: General interior lighting

Cue 10   **Chris**: "... we can get round Marie."   (Page 34)
              Black-out

ACT I, Scene 6

To open: Semi-darkness

Cue 11   When ready   (Page 34)
              Flash of lightning

Cue 12   Music of evil-doing plays   (Page 34)
              A full moon rises in the sky

Cue 13   **Everyone**: (*singing*) *"LAND!"*   (Page 44)
              Black-out

ACT II, Scene 1

To open: Darkness

Cue 14   **Female voice on tannoy**: "... from Knapeley WI." (Page 45)
              Harsh spotlight on lectern

Cue 15   **Annie** walks up to the lectern   (Page 45)
              Green light on traffic-light warning system

Cue 16   **Annie**: "Skipton Gen —— "   (Page 45)
              Green light changes to amber

Cue 17   **Annie**: "*My* John..." Pause   (Page 46)
           Amber light changes to red

Cue 18   **Chris**: "...singing 'Jerusalem'."   (Page 46)
           Sudden snap back to full light

ACT II, SCENE 2

To open: General interior lighting

No cues

ACT II, SCENE 3

To open: General interior lighting

Cue 19   **Ruth** poses   (Page 51)
           Flashguns to indicate camera flashes from off stage

Cue 20   **Annie** poses   (Page 51)
           Flashgun

Cue 21   **Jessie** and **Cora** pose   (Page 52)
           Flashgun

Cue 22   **Celia** catwalks out with natural aplomb   (Page 52)
           Several flashes

Cue 23   **Chris** gently turns the wreath so that it reads "WOW"   (Page 52)
           Colossal volley of flashes goes off

Cue 24   **Chris** goes out   (Page 53)
           Black-out

ACT II, SCENE 4

To open: Functional, unglamorous overhead striplights

Cue 25   **Jessie**: "... 'it never quite did.'"   (Page 60)
           Fade Lights. Spotlights on girls picking up letters

ACT II, SCENE 5

To open: General interior lighting

No cues

Act II, Scene 6

To open: General interior lighting

Cue 26	**Liam**: "Let there be light!" *Very bright lights come on*	(Page 69)
Cue 27	**Chris**: "Right. OK. I hadn't realized." *After a beat a ferocious key light comes on*	(Page 71)

Act II, Scene 7

To open: General interior lighting

No cues

Act II, Scene 8

To open: Exterior lighting, summer

Cue 28	**Chris** and **Annie** look at the sunflowers swaying in the breeze *Black-out*	(Page 78)

EFFECTS PLOT

ACT I

Cue 13	**Lawrence** exits *Music stops*	(Page 35)
Cue 14	**Lawrence** takes the photo of **Celia** *Loud sound of a camera light*	(Page 39)
Cue 15	**Lawrence** takes the photo of **Cora** *Loud sound of a camera light*	(Page 40)
Cue 16	**Lawrence** takes the photo of **Jessie** *Loud sound of a camera light*	(Page 40)
Cue 17	**Lawrence** takes the photo of **Annie** *Loud sound of a camera light*	(Page 41)
Cue 18	**Lawrence** takes the photo of **Ruth** *Loud sound of a camera light*	(Page 42)
Cue 19	**Lawrence** takes the photo of **Chris** *Loud sound of a camera light, then music: an R&B version of "Jerusalem"*	(Page 43)
Cue 20	**Chris**: "... I think it's time to ..." *The music builds*	(Page 44)

ACT II

Cue 21	**Annie**: "Skipton Gen —— " *A buzz*	(Page 45)
Cue 22	**Annie**: "*My* John ..." Pause *Short buzz sounds*	(Page 46)
Cue 23	**Cora**: "Prepare for a life on the internet." *Car horn outside*	(Page 48)
Cue 24	To open SCENE 3 *Music plays briefly*	(Page 49)
Cue 25	**Annie**: "... he would have understood in a second." *Music plays*	(Page 59)
Cue 26	**Jessie**: "... she'd tried everything else —— " *Music gets louder*	(Page 60)
Cue 27	**Everyone**: "Chris! STEADY-Y! (*Etc.*) *Music stops*	(Page 61)

Cue 28	**Chris** exits *Music plays: "Jerusalem"*	(Page 73)
Cue 29	**Annie**: "I absolve you, my child." *Music plays*	(Page 77)
Cue 30	**Annie**: "Go and get some chips." *Music plays*	(Page 78)

A licence issued by Samuel French Ltd to perform this play does not include permission to use the Incidental music specified in this copy. Where the place of performance is already licensed by the PERFORMING RIGHT SOCIETY a return of the music used must be made to them. If the place of performance is not so licensed then application should be made to the Performing Right Society, 29 Berners Street, London W1T 3AB (website: www.mcps-prs-alliance.co.uk).

A separate and additional licence from PHONOGRAPHIC PERFORMANCE LTD, 1 Upper James Street, London W1F 9DE (website: www.ppluk.com) is needed whenever commercial recordings are used.